...and the snow came up to here...
SCHOOLS of
CARLTON COUNTY
MINNESOTA

Nancy C. Hanson

Nancy C. Hanson

Dedicated to...

the teachers of ungraded one-room schools
in Carlton County

With thanks to...

Moose Lake Area Historical Society
Carlton County Historical Society
Minnesota Historical Society
Marlene Wisuri
Joe Malkovich
Betty Lehet
Christine Carlson
Dan Reed

and with thanks for the work of
John Manni
Ed Manni

Copyright © 2011 Nancy C. Hanson

ISBN 978-0-9765890-6-8

Published by the author with the assistance of
Dovetailed Press LLC
5263 North Shore Drive
Duluth, MN 55804

For additional copies, contact
Nancy C. Hanson
3906 Maple Drive
Barnum, MN 55707-9794
218.389.3423

Front Cover design: Rose Kuhlman
Book layout & design: Marlene Wisuri
Printed and bound in the United States of America

Photo caption key:
MLAHS - Moose Lake Area Historical Society
CCHS - Carlton County Historical Society
Photos used with permission.

Cover photos: Right center, Kettle River students, 1929-30; Middle 2nd from top, Bjorklund school and students
photos Author's Collection

Title page: Students at Cromwell School, 1902
CCHS photo

TABLE of CONTENTS ✏

Moose Lake 8th grade graduates, 1913
MLAHS photo

PREFACE ___✎

Writing the history of rural schools, even for a geographical area as small as Carlton County, Minnesota, can be a challenging and complicated matter. The Native Americans who first inhabited the area taught their children largely through oral tradition, storytelling, and example. When white settlers moved in, their children were often taught, first in homes and later in one-room schools, sometimes roughly constructed of logs. Because of the difficulties of transportation, it was necessary for schools to be close to the families they served. This resulted in many small schools that often burned, were moved, or later consolidated. Tracing such a fluid history, without many written records and when name changes or the use of two or more names for a single school were common, becomes difficult at best. Further complicating Carlton County history is the fact that the area suffered massive and destructive forest fires on October 12, 1918. Along with the loss of over 500 lives, over 4,000 homes, and over 6,000 barns; 41 school buildings were also burned. Many of these schools were not rebuilt following the fires.

Nancy Hanson has spent many years collecting school history through documents, newspaper stories, photographs, previously published works, and interviews. She assembled her research into several albums of notes, documents, memorabilia, letters, and photographs, which are now condensed and presented in this volume. Her work was further organized and supplemented by research done by Joseph Malkovich during an internship at the Carlton County Historical Society in the summer of 2001. Joe's work was funded by a grant from the Gerin-Fahlstrom Educational Fund of the Carlton County Historical Society Foundation and some of his research is incorporated here.

This volume of Carlton County school history is not meant to be a definitive history, but rather an overview and summary of information currently available. The files of the Carlton County Historical Society and the Moose Lake Area Historical Society contain many additional records and are open to researchers wishing a more complete history of individual schools and communities. Judging by the sheer number of schools listed in this work, it is obvious that education was of great importance to the people of Carlton County.

Marlene Wisuri,
Publisher and Director Emerita, Carlton County Historical Society

Note: In the course of Joe Malkovich's research work, numerous questionnaires were distributed to former Carlton County students and teachers. You will find short quotations from these questionnaires scattered throughout this book, titled a *student* or *teacher remembers....*

AN INTRODUCTION ✎

There has always been interest in schools, good memories and bad. We share them. This is obvious when we see people flock to reunions. Histories are written, pictures and mementos are collected to commemorate the event.

I am an historian and genealogist. While working on local history I discovered how important the school is to the community. In small towns the school *is* the town. Try to make a controversial decision concerning the school and everyone has an opinion.

PATIENCE AND SELF-DENIAL

Elements of social and moral science were some of the qualities required by the legislature in 1881. They included industry, economy, punctuality, patience, self-denial, health, purity, temperance, cleanliness, honesty, truth, justice, politeness, philanthropy, patriotism, self-respect, perseverance, cheerfulness, courage, self-reliance, gratitude, mercy, and kindness.

In 1860 the high school curriculum in St. Anthony (Minneapolis), Minnesota, included physical geography, algebra, geography, surveying, trigonometry, Latin, Greek, chemistry, and orthography (perfect spelling) for good measure. Attendance was mandatory. This list appears challenging regardless of the grade level.

In the early days, if they could read and write, immigrants taught their own children. Often the Bible was the only book in the house. Food and shelter were the priorities. After homes were built and as new settlers arrived, they began to organize churches and schools.

After the village was founded, the neighbors often banded together to hire a school master. This was often the preacher or a respected resident. School was held in homes or churches—in the native language of course. If there were several languages spoken by students it must have been difficult. Eventually a school was built, often of logs with a dirt floor. Dirt floors were the first blackboards. Backless recitation benches preceded desks. There were a few spellers and readers and the occasional slate. Eventually students had paper and goose quill pens which had to be sharpened by the teacher. Ink would often freeze in the winter.

An unidentified Carlton County log school house, 1891. photo Author's Collection

The railroads brought rapid construction and immigration. Before public funding schools often were on a subscription basis costing one or two dollars a month per student and the teacher boarded around. Eventually a majority of freeholders would petition the county commissioners to form a school district. Commissioners had the power to allocate school district land from each section for the financing of public schools. Counties had no taxable income to support schools and districts were formally organized under a state board of education. The first elected board of education was January 25, 1919. As people began to homestead they often donated land for schools and churches. These often had the name of the land holder. Children attended school as farm seasons allowed and chores permitted, usually two or three month terms. The compulsory school attendance law came into being in 1885.

In 1861 there were already 456 schools in Minnesota of which 235 were log. Schools were built every few miles depending on population needs. Children often walked a mile or more through the woods as there were few roads. Eventually there were horse drawn school busses. Some districts even offered commuter service to pick up points. Sometimes children would carry a baked potato in their pockets for warmth and lunch.

"LICKEN AND LEARNIN" GO TOGETHER

In the 1860s and 70s, if a professional teacher was hired, it was often a single man who came out west because he was incompetent, drank too much, or was involved in a scandal out east. Pay was low and so was prestige. There was a high turnover. A man who failed at everything else got himself a birch rod and became a teacher. Corporal punishment was the rule and considered healthy and indispensable. A box or cuff on the ears was considered healthy when in fact it often led to infections and deafness.

Teachers at the Ronkainen School,
photo Author's Collection

TEACHERS

Young women teachers soon became the norm at least until they married. Teaching attracted women who lacked other professional opportunities. Pay was poor but it did offer a certain amount of prestige for a woman. By 1900 teachers earned $40-50 month and boarded in private homes. Board was usually $5 to $10 a month. Most teachers I have talked to found satisfaction in teaching even though they could not be engaged or married. This law later changed and married women were allowed to teach.

PROUD TO BE A TEACHER

In the early days anyone completing the 8th grade and meeting minimum qualifications, including an examination, could teach in rural districts. Some schools had teacher training courses which would prepare a student to teach the lower grades. I have heard so many elderly people say they only had an 8th grade education. That is all there was in rural schools. Students wanting a four year high school degree had to complete 8th grade and pass a state board examination. The biggest problem was finding transportation to a larger school.

NORMAL SCHOOL

Normal school was teacher college. One and two year satisfactory completion got a student a teaching certificate to teach in ungraded rural schools. By 1890, 20% of normal school applicants had a high school diploma. The first normal school was founded at Winona in 1858. Normal schools were established at Mankato in 1868; St. Cloud in 1869; Superior, WI in 1893; University of Minnesota in 1869; Moorhead in 1888; and Duluth in 1902. Graduate courses, as they were called, offered an elementary certificate which took one year, and an advanced degree in two years. There was also a three year certificate. After two years of teaching they were awarded a life two year certificate. Most teachers eventually got their four year degree.

State Normal School in Duluth. This school later became the University of Minnesota Duluth. CCHS photo

HOW CHILDREN LIVED IN THE EARLY DAYS OF CARLTON COUNTY

Children were usually part of a large family. My great-great grandmother had 22 children, no twins. They all survived. It was common to have a baby every year or two. If there are a gaps in recorded birth dates a child probably died. Mortality was high. I have a relative who lost six children to cholera.

Our grandmother married a widower who had six children and then had six more of her own. We often asked her what they all did for fun. She said, "All we did was work." Children were needed to work the farm. Often more than one generation lived together.

I am sure they found time for fun. One thing they all seem to remember was making maple sugar in the spring. They got to spread it on the snow and make candy. Molasses was also used. Just playing was a treat for children. Sundays were supposed to be a day of rest. Children were to be quiet with no shouting or running about. They should read the Bible or other books and eat simple food.

Getting to school was a challenge in winter. Just walking the mile or two to school was hard. Horse drawn school busses eventually came on the scene, which made things easier. The busses were still cold despite foot warmers. Horse and buggies were usually used for special events like sleigh rides and to church. An old school bus is on display at the Carlton County Fair Grounds.

Men and women aged early from hard labor, accidents and illness. Joints and backs got stiff. It seems like a hard life to us, but that was all they knew.

Despite all this they had the satisfaction of accomplishment.

"AND THE SNOW CAME UP TO HERE"

The one room school house is charming to reflect on, but it was a difficult life. The teacher or a student had to get to school early to heat the building with a pot bellied stove. Some teachers were innovative and had the students bring a stick of wood for the fire every day. Some teachers required a load of wood for each child. Wood stoves were not effective heaters. It was too hot by the stove and too cold away from it. The snow often blew in under the door. Teachers usually walked to school and the teacher and community were responsible for maintenance. Students hauled water and they used a common dipper. The out house was in back of course. Most students never complained of being cold. Lunch was brought in a lard pail, which often contained the makings for a soup to which everyone contributed.

Think about it. One room with up to forty-five students age four to eighteen. Most people say that the one room school offered a sound education with lots of review and practice for the older children and enrichment for the younger. Schools were usually about one to two miles apart. As populations grew, larger schools were built and consolidations began. This was always controversial and required many referendums before the issue was passed. After the 1918 fire, the life of the one room school began to end due to forced consolidations as the state did not allow enough money for small districts to rebuild.

It was sometimes said one room schools trained the voice not the mind and that the 3R's were force fed. Thinking was discouraged in favor of rote memorizing and penmanship before all else. How many of us still remember some of those poems we memorized like *Hiawatha* and *The Wreck of the Hesperus* and the good penmanship? We could all still use some of that. Often with today's curriculums, teachers are told exactly what to teach. In Carlton County, ungraded school districts had a county superintendent of school, a system that many wish would return. The superintendent would visit all of the schools on a rotation basis. Many remember Miss Nilsen and her snowmobile—a converted Model T. The superintendents and their years of service were Minna Walker (1898-1900), Reverend Nils Nilsen (1900-1913), Nora Nilsen (1913-1934), Louise Swenson (1934-1962), and Robert Anderson (1962-1967).

Carlton County had 48 school districts at one time. Now there are only 7 with the same number of superintendents.

Rev. Nils Nilsen, Carlton County School Superintendent 1900-1913. MLAHS photo

Nora Nilsen, county superintendent 1913-1934, pictured with her snowmobile, 1920. MLAHS photo

RURAL AND UNIFIED SCHOOL DISTRICTS and SCHOOLS
DATES OF ORGANIZATION ✏

1. THOMSON/ESKO   October 4, 1870
    THOMSON
    KAANTA
    PANTSAR
    OTILLA (GRANT)
    TWEITH (NELS JOHNSON)
    HUOT
    MAUNU (JEFFERSON)
    FORBAY
    WONGSTEDT
    WASHINGTON
    LINCOLN
    WINTERQUIST

2. CARLTON   September 18, 1871
    CARLTON
    TWIN LAKES TOWNSHIP:
    IVERSON
    LONE PINE
    PLEASANT VIEW

3. MOOSE LAKE   March 11, 1873

4. SANDY LAKE   November 7, 1874

5. MAHTOWA   October 25, 1875

6. BARNUM   March 1, 1880

7. CLOQUET   January 4, 1881

8. CENTRAL/NEMADJI   March 15, 1881
    CENTRAL
    CONNOR
    HUFFMAN'S CORNERS
    BENNY PETERSON

9. WRENSHALL (Pleasant Valley)   December 13, 1884
    Dissolved and annexed to #15 August 3, 1937

10. GUNDERSON July 8, 1885

A group of students, ND
CCHS photo

GUNDERSON
MUDD CREEK (1893)
PICKEREL LAKE (LOST SCHOOL)

11. WRIGHT   November 13, 1886

12. AUTOMBA   September 20, 1888
    AUTOMBA
    BJORKLUND
    JOKIMAKI
    ERICKSON
    MICHAELSON
    KARLSON
    ECKMAN
    SANDBLOM

13. CROMWELL   June 17, 1891
    CROMWELL TOWNSHIP:
        CROMWELL
        BECK
    RED CLOVER TOWNSHIP:
        SWANSON
        ASHLEY
        WALKER

14. SAWYER   January 30, 1893
    DITCHBANK
    PARK LAKE

15. WRENSHALL January 2, 1894
    WRENSHALL
    PLEASANT VALLEY
    PRAEFKE
    MCKINLEY
    BARKER

16. KALEVALA   July 30, 1894
    KALEVALA
    MANSIKKA
    SALO (RANUA)
    BJORKLUND
    HOLMI-KOSTER (NASI)
    HOKKANEN
    NORDBERG/STENMAN
    JOKIMAKI

Louise Swenson, Carlton County School
Superintendent, 1934-1962.
CCHS photo

11

KONSTI
AUTOMBA TOWNSHIP:
    ERICKSON
    CARLSON

17. SELGREN   January 8, 1895
    Consolidated with #6 August 10, 1910

18. SAWYER   February 11, 1895

19. ATKINSON   January 7, 1896
    OTTER CREEK

20. SKELTON   January 7, 1896
    Consolidated with #6 August 10, 1910

21. EAGLE LAKE   January 13, 1896

22. MUNSON   September 13, 1897

23. HUFFMAN'S CORNERS   November 13, 1899
    Consolidated with #8 June 29, 1911

24. SPENSER   January 8, 1901
    Consolidated with #6 April 29, 1919

25. KETTLE RIVER   June 10, 1901
    MCKINLEY (RONKAINEN)
    PAAPANEN
    MICHAELSON
    ECKMAN
    BIRCH GROVE (SANDBLOM)
    KETTLE RIVER

26. BESEMAN   June 9, 1902
    BESEMAN TOWNSHIP:
        CENTER (1912)
        NORTON
        NILSEN (BRENNICK) (1912)
    LAKEVIEW TOWNSHIP:
        LAKESIDE
        LINCOLN
        RIVERSIDE (SOUTH) (WALIMAA)

27. SCANLON   July 14, 1902

A. L. Winterquist, Esko Schools superintendent 1919-1945. CCHS photo

12

28. CORONA   August 10, 1903

29. BEEHIVE   September 14, 1903
    Consolidated with #8 June 29, 1911

30. BENNY PETERSON   November 9, 1903   Consolidated with #13

31. CLEAR CREEK   November 14, 1904

32. HOLYOKE   January 3, 1905
    HOLYOKE SOUTHSIDE
    HOLYOKE TOWN SCHOOL

33. CLEAR CREEK   July 12, 1909   Consolidated with #13

34. SPLIT ROCK   October 3, 1910
    JOHNSON (1915)
    WILSON (1915), SHUSTA
    LINCOLN (1915), SOBELESKI
    WASHINGTON #3
    KACHINSKI

35. LONE PINE, HANSON   November 6, 1911

36. BLACKHOOF VALLEY   July 14, 1913

37. SILVER, BIRCH GROVE   August 1, 1916
    Consolidated with #3 October 27, 1936
    BIRCH GROVE (SANDBLOM)

38. BLACKHOOF, RIVERSIDE   August 7, 1917

39. LAKESIDE   February 4, 1919

40. BARKER   November 4, 1919   Dissolved, annexed to #15

41. SOUTHSIDE HOLYOKE   November 4, 1919

42. WATSON   December 7, 1920

43. PARK LAKE   October 7, 1921

44. CLEAR CREEK   February 7, 1922   Dissolved October 5, 1937?
    RAYMOND, SOPER 1937

45. (HOLYOKE) FOXBORO, EAST PUGSLEY   March 6, 1923

46. PERCH LAKE, BERGMAN   July 9, 1923

47. BLACKHOOF   September 4, 1923

48. UNORGANIZED 48
        BIG LAKE
        KATTMAN
        DITCH BANK
        BERGMAN
        LINCOLN
        FOND DU LAC RESERVATION DAY SCHOOL
        NORMANTOWN DAY SCHOOL

CONSOLIDATED SCHOOL DISTRICTS:

BARNUM 91
CARLTON 93
CLOQUET 94
CROMWELL 95
MOOSE LAKE 97
ESKO 99

Students at the Cromwell grade school, CCHS photo

NORMAL TRAINING CLASS

Miss Mabel Reid, Instructor

Martha Almer Elsie Nelson
Mamie Juntunen Emelia Nicholson
Martha Lindquist Joan Powers
Esther Longsyo

Normal School pages from the Cloquet High School *White Pine*, 1921 and 1923, CCHS photos

Teachers Training

For an efficient teacher, good-training is vital.

The state department of education, realizing this necessity, has established approximately one hundred teachers' training departments in Minnesota.

Cloquet, which is always foremost in the progress of education, offered this course for the first time in 1915. It was given every year under the instruction of Miss Emma Williamson, but in 1918, on account of the great conflagration of October 12th, it had to be discontinued for that term.

The training was again resumed at the L. F. Leach school in the fall of 1919. Up to the present time there have been seventy-two graduates, of which 50 per cent are still teaching in rural communities.

This department is entirely supported by the state. It is really the only vocational department in the high school. At the end of the year's work, the graduates are presented with a first class teacher's certificate, which enables them to fulfill positions of first grade teachers in rural communities.

This year we entered the L. F. Leach school with Miss Mabel Reid as instructor. During the first semester, however, we spent two months in the basement of the Garfield school, giving our room to the Junior high school.

The class of 1921 consists of Esther Longsyo, Elsie Nelson, Emelia Nicholson, Martha Almer, Martha Lindquist, Joan Powers, Mamie Juntunen.

Thus, we, the future teachers (?) have tried to learn by our mistakes and we can safely say that the bee who gets the honey does not loaf around the hive. We know that experienced teachers practice what they preach, but during this course we have merely preached what we've practiced. Above all we have learned to love our work and know our duty as teachers. We realize now that there are no shady trees or hammocks scattered along the road to success. Furthermore,

"I am glad I am a school teacher,
With pencil and book and rule,
To teach the young ideas to shoot,
And extirpate the fool.
The heights of knowledge I point out,
And upward lead the way.
And with my pupils pressing on
I'm happy all the day."
—Mamie Juntunen.

NORMAL TRAINING CLASS

Class and high schools from which graduated:

Julia Bertram	Cloquet	Cloquet H. S., '22
Theresa Chalupsky	Barnum	New Progue H. S., '20
Lydia Hiukka	Thomson	Lincoln H. S., '22
Alice Jensen	Cloquet	Cloquet H. S., '22
Elizabeth Josselyn	Barnum	Barnum H. S., '20
Cecelia Kipp	Barnum	Barnum H. S., '21
Hilda Lyngen	Moose Lake	Moose Lake H. S., '21
Mildred Nelson	Cloquet	Cloquet H. S., '21
Harold Olson	Sebeka	Cloquet H. S., '22

Seven years ago a Normal Training Department was started in the Cloquet High School. Up to the present, eighty-four students have completed the course and have earned Teacher's Certificates of the first class,

1923

Teachers remember...

"I taught for 30 years. If you got married you lost your job, so I stayed home 15 years and raised my family."

"I became a teacher because I loved children. The pay was poor, but we survived."

CARLTON COUNTY MAPS

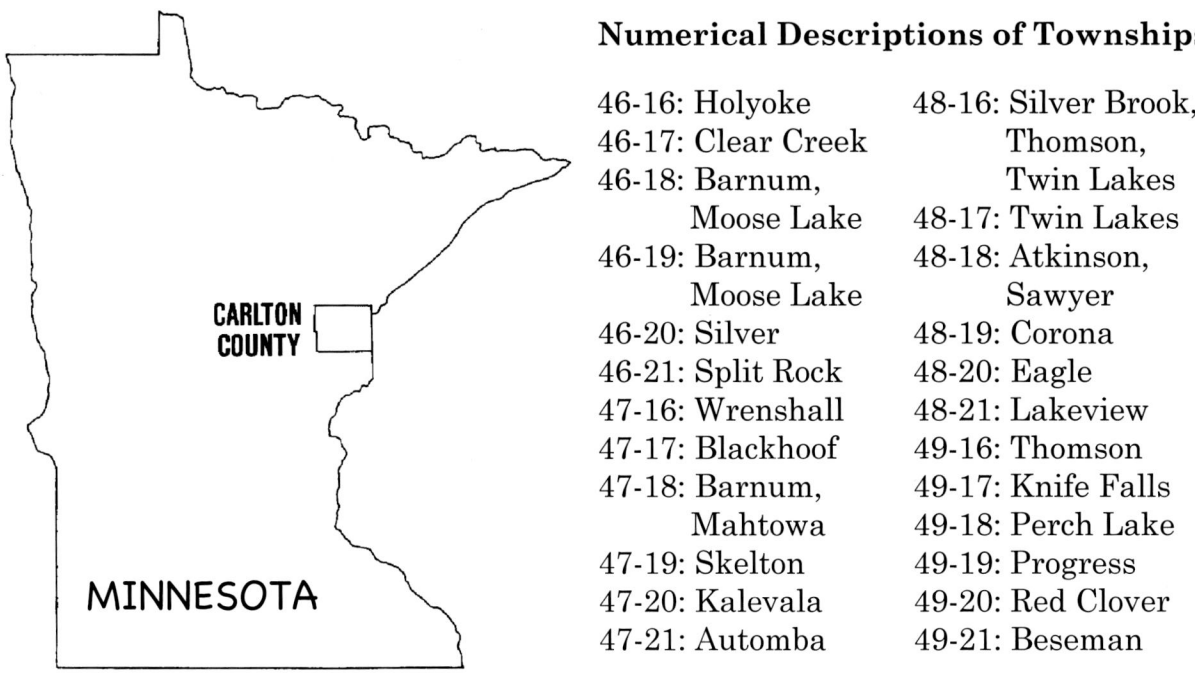

Numerical Descriptions of Townships

46-16: Holyoke
46-17: Clear Creek
46-18: Barnum,
    Moose Lake
46-19: Barnum,
    Moose Lake
46-20: Silver
46-21: Split Rock
47-16: Wrenshall
47-17: Blackhoof
47-18: Barnum,
    Mahtowa
47-19: Skelton
47-20: Kalevala
47-21: Automba

48-16: Silver Brook,
    Thomson,
    Twin Lakes
48-17: Twin Lakes
48-18: Atkinson,
    Sawyer
48-19: Corona
48-20: Eagle
48-21: Lakeview
49-16: Thomson
49-17: Knife Falls
49-18: Perch Lake
49-19: Progress
49-20: Red Clover
49-21: Beseman

Carlton County, Minnesota

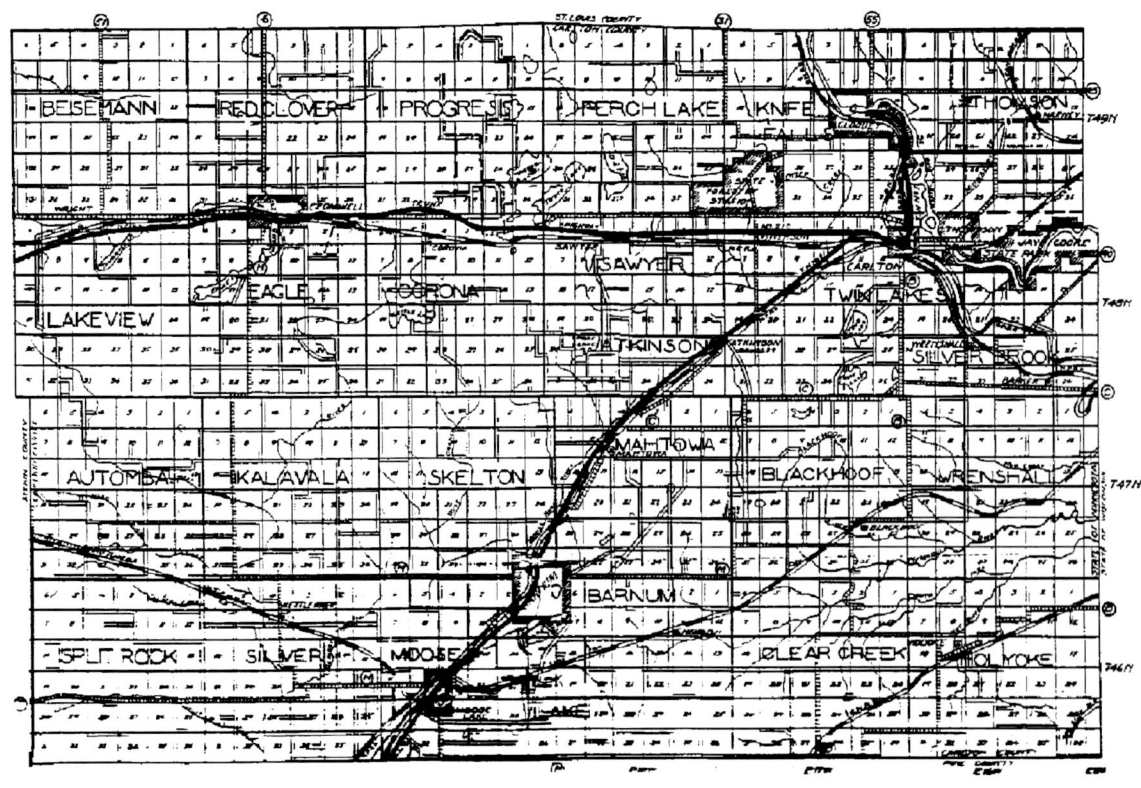

SCHOOL DISTRICTS IN 1948

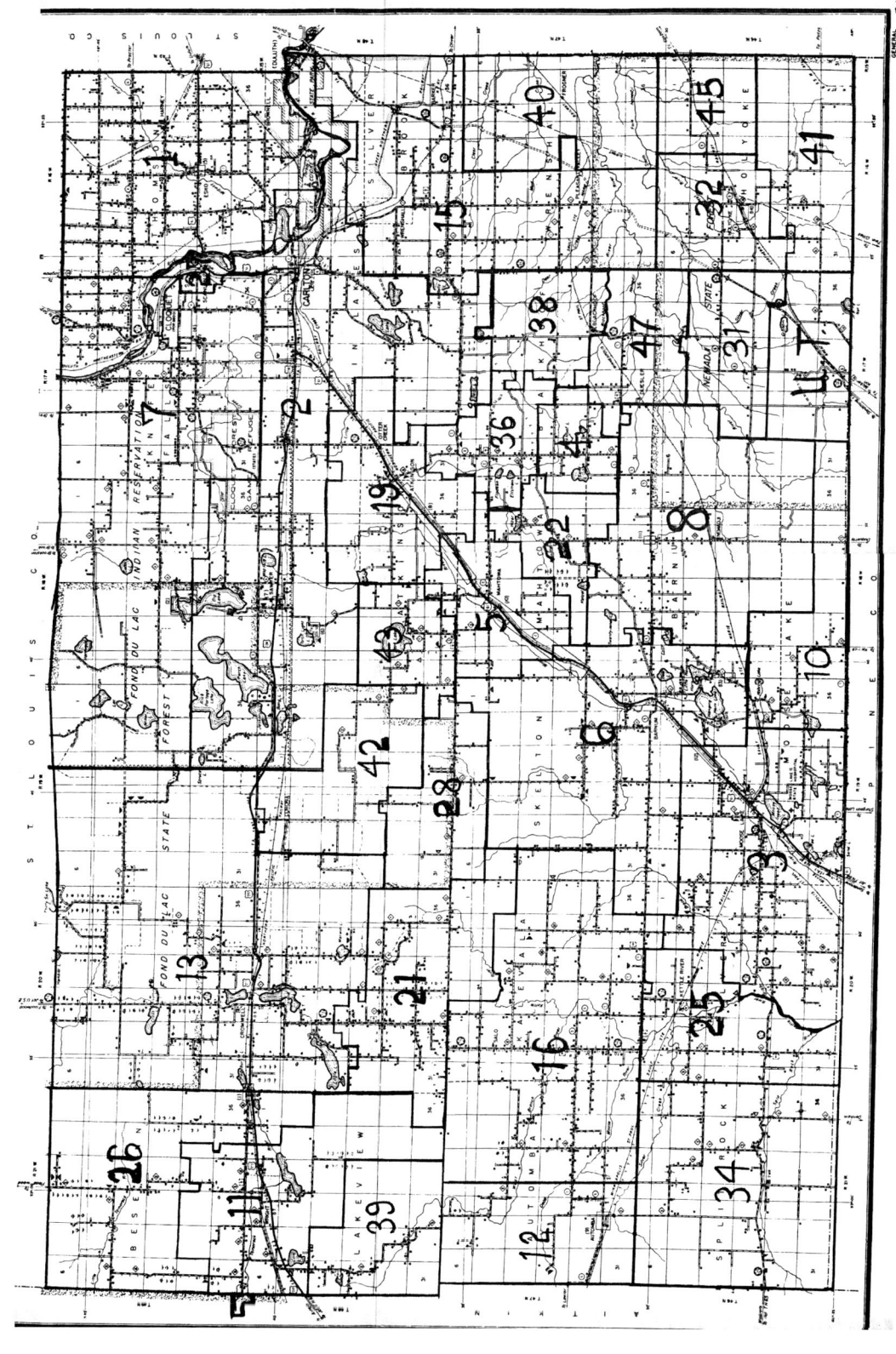

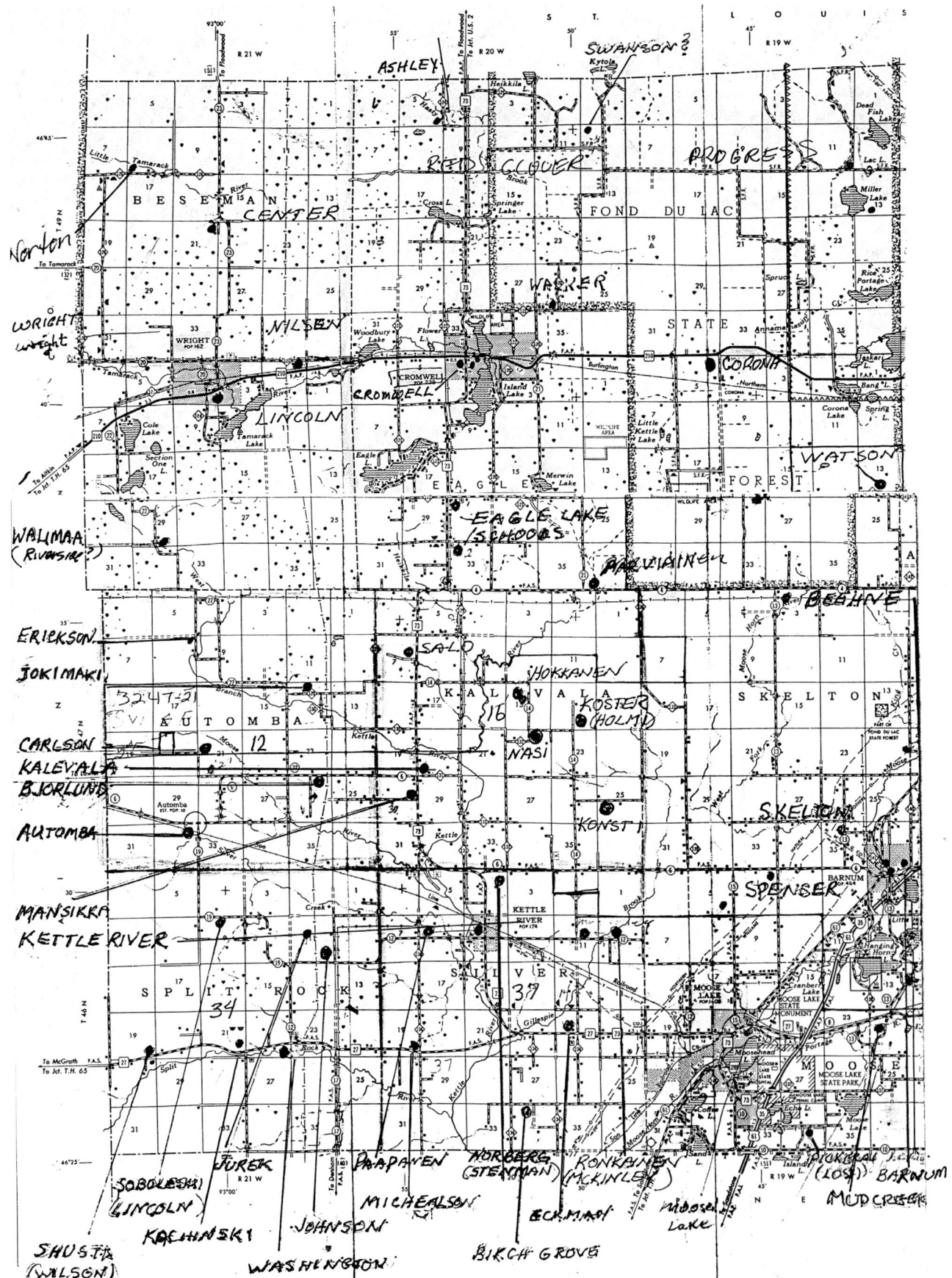

18

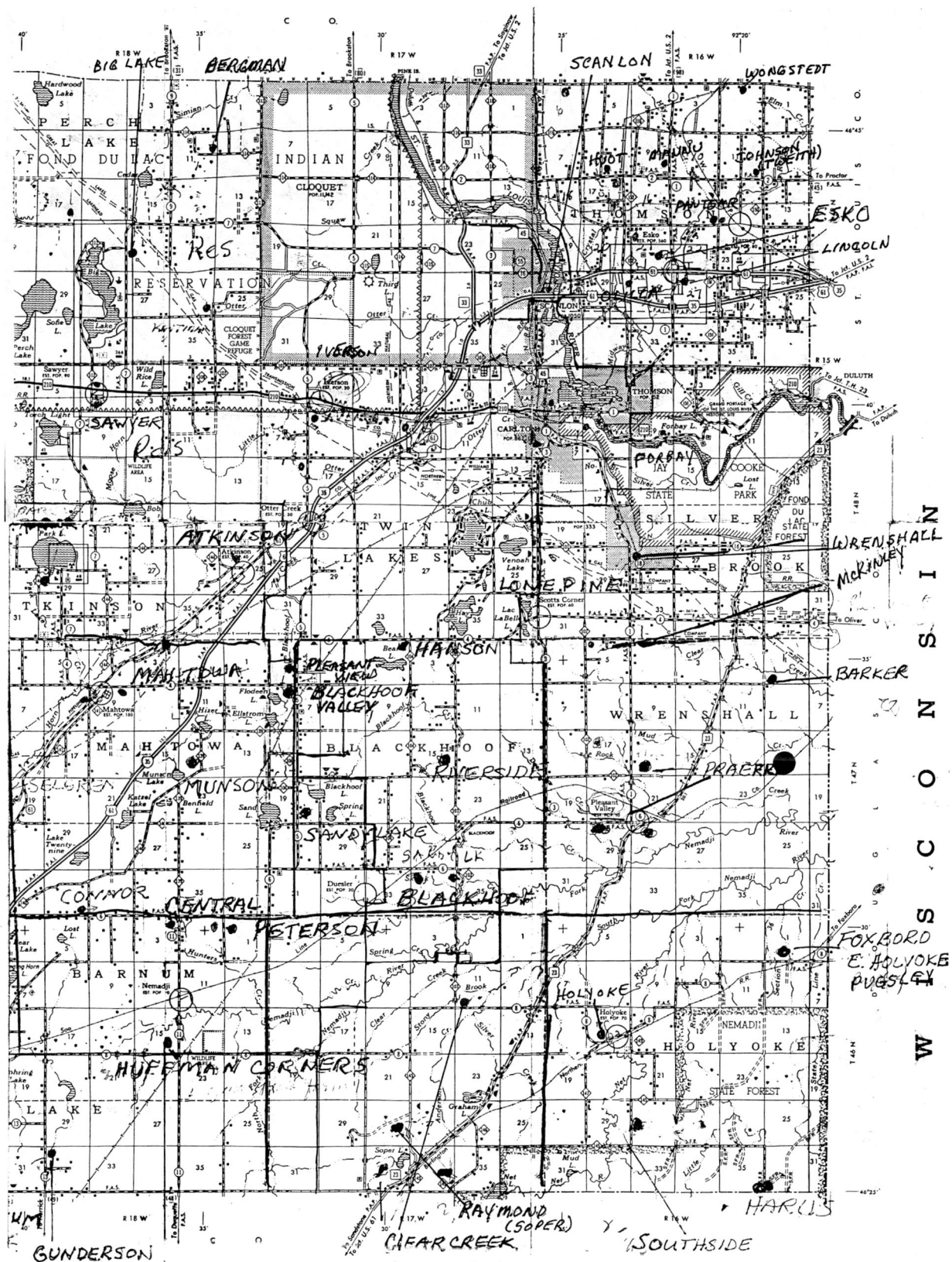

Carlton County School Locations

maps Author's Collection

TEACHERS IN THE UNGRADED SCHOOLS
IN CARLTON COUNTY 1933-34

Louise A. Swenson, Superintendent

DISTRICT	TEACHER	SCHOOL	ADDRESS
4	Beth Dahlin	Sandy Lake	Barnum
5	Adah Carlson, Principal	Mahtowa	Mahtowa
	Mary Ballou		
8	J. J. Leipzig, Principal	Central	Barnum
	Veda Leonard		
	Inez Johnson		
	Lillian Frazer		
9	Eva Harris	Praefke	Wrenshall
10	Inez Almquist, Principal	Mud Creek	Moose Lake
	Ella Swanson, Principal	Gunderson	Moose Lake
11	R. Leroy Ewoldsen, Principal	Wright	Wright
	Louis Leipold		
	Fern Kunkle		
	Aadla Laulay		
12	Florence Peters	Automba	Automba
16	Walma Johnson, Principal	Kalevala	Kettle River
	Lyla Johnson		
	Aili Siltanen		
	Ellen Hallonen		
	Alice Latvala		
	Dagmar Miettinen		
19	Carl Anderson, Principal	Atkinson	Atkinson
	Dorothy Brooks		
21	Martha Maki, Principal	Eagle Lake	Cromwell
	Linnea Jarvi		
	Irene Holmes		
	Irene Isaacson		
22	Viola Gulliford	Munson	Barnum
25	Ruth Soderberg, Principal	Kettle River	Kettle River
	Inez Fraser		
	Ethel Emilson		
26	Hilda Olson	Central	Wright
	Elvera Larson	Nilsen	Wright
27	Olive Bayless, Principal	Scanlon	Scanlon
	Elsa Anderson		
	Helen Otteson		
28	Florence Torvick	Beehive	Mahtowa
32	Nora Olson, Principal	Holyoke	Holyoke
	Bertha Beckman		

34	Gladys Flattum	Johnson	Kettle River
	Stephanie Majewski	Wilson	Arthyde
	Ida Johnson	Lincoln	Kettle River
	Mary Ceryance	Washington	Kettle River
35	Katherine Schauland, Principal	Blackhoof Valley	Carlton
	Lucille Tyman		
37	Grace Putzke	Birch Grove	Moose Lake
	Hilda Carlson	McKinley	Moose Lake
38	Selmer Stromme	Lakeside	Tamarack
40	Helen Nelson	Barker	Wrenshall
41	Myrtella Lindberg	Southside	Holyoke
42	Beth Swanson	Watson	Sawyer
43	Alma Bentfield	Park Lake	Mahtowa
44	Florence Hedberg	Raymond	Nickerson
45	Mrs. Clem Lull	Foxboro	Holyoke
46	Bertha Johnson	Bergman	Cloquet
47	Mable Larson	Blackhoof	Barnum
Un.	May Beattie	Big Lake	Cloquet
	Freda Mathison, Principal	Sawyer	Sawyer

Maggie Yeager, Carlton County teacher
photos Author's Collection

A TYPICAL DAY IN A ONE ROOM SCHOOL
As Recalled by Teacher Esther Swanson

9:00 – 9:15	Opening Exercises
9:15 – 10:15	Reading, grades 1-8
10:15 – 10:30	Recess
10:30 – 11:30	Arithmetic, grades 1-8
11:30 – 12:00	History
12:00 – 1:00	Lunch Hour
1:00 – 1:15	Music
1:15 – 1:45	Geography, grades 3-8
1:45 – 2:00	Penmanship, Palmer Method
2:00 – 2:30	Reading, grades 1-4
2:30 – 3:00	Language
3:00 – 3:30	Spelling
3:30 – 3:45	Science or Civics
3:45 – 4:00	Duties and Dismissal

Subjects like reading and arithmetic would be taught in a rolling fashion, so the teacher world spend some part of the time with every grade level, giving them a different lesson. Esther felt that penmanship was an important element of early education that has been lost. She also elucidated the "Duties" time period—at the end of the day the teacher would assign the students chores, like clapping erasers, wiping of the boards, watering the plants, dusting, cleaning, and straightening up in general.

The top seven discipline problems in public schools in 1940...
1. Talking
2. Chewing gum
3. Making noise
4. Running in the halls
5. Getting out of turn in line.
6. Wearing improper clothes
7. Not putting paper in wastebaskets

ONE ROOM SCHOOL

Down from the ridges, up from the dales,
They come with their lard-bucket dinner pails,
Filled with sandwich of egg, sausage, and cake
Or some other tidbit that mother would bake.

In gingham and overalls, mud on their feet,
They walked the wood floor, two to a seat;
Though all from the country, close to the loam,
Each showed use of soap and work of the comb.

From six to sixteen, all in one room,
With just one to weave this human cloth loom;
Though often it seemed like Bedlam and worse,
We learned the three R's by rote and by verse.

Chalk and the blackboards, map on the wall,
Outdoor "privies" for nature's cold call,
Seem primitive today as a way to gain knowledge,
Believe it or not, some went to college!
It's good to remember, I would not forget,
Country schools of the past, we owe each a debt;
Through good times and bad, depression and boom,
My thoughts often stray to eight grades in a room!

Author Unknown

DISTRICTS & SCHOOLS

DISTRICT 1 - THOMSON TOWNSHIP
Silver Brook, SE Thomson NE Twin Lakes (5-48-16)

Second Thomson School
CCHS photo by Smith Studios

The first school district in Carlton County was organized in 1870, but the first school was not built until 1885— a one room frame building in the village of Thomson, which was also used at times as a church and court house. The village was settled in 1869 and was the county seat until 1889. In 1871 William Shaw became the first county superintendent. Ella Owen was the first teacher. By 1908 the district had a semi-graded school with three teachers located just west of the first school. It was the first school in Esko. In 1912 Carlton took in the village of Thomson and in 1913 Iverson was incorporated. There were eventually nine schoolhouses in the district but many were lost in the 1918 Fires. These schools were replaced by the brick Washington and Lincoln schools.

Thomson School students, early 1900s, CCHS photo

DISTRICT 1 - RURAL THOMSON

KAANTA (NE-NE-35-49-18) The school was built in 1887 and located where Helberg and Nynas Road intersect in section 35. It did not burn in the 1918 fire. Schools that did not burn in the fire were used for classes between 1918 and 1920 when the Washington and Lincoln schools were being built. Churches and the town hall were also used. Kaanta and the other schools that hadn't burned were closed by 1920 when the new schools opened.

PANTSAR (WASHINGTON) (SE-SE-15-49-16) This school was probably the first school built outside of Thomson village in 1885. The school was built on Isaac Raattamaa's land. This school burned in 1887 and another school was built on the S.W corner of the N. O. Olson land. It did not burn in 1918. Later the building was moved to the present site of the Esko Insurance Building parking lot where it was used as a store building. Anna Swanson Hultman was a teacher around 1903.

Pantsar School, CCHS photo

OTILLA (GRANT) (SE-NE 29-49-16) 1887-1920. It is not known for sure if the school burned or not in 1918.

TWEITH (NELS JOHNSON) (SE-SE–11-49-16) at Erickson and North Cloquet Road. It was built post 1887 and existed after 1900. According to Ed Sunnarborg and Charlie Johnson the school burned in the 1918 fire and was not rebuilt.

Maunu School students first through eighth grades, 1904, CCHS photo

HUOT (SW-SE-8-49-16) North Cloquet Road and Erkilla Road. It burned in the 1918 fires.

MAUNU (JEFFERSON) (NE-SE-48-16) Canosia and Forstie Road.
Teacher Hilder Swensen Archer said, "(It was a) one room school near Esko's Corners were I taught September 1907 to May 1908. All were Finnish but one family, the Johnsons, with whom I stayed."

FORBAY (JAY COOKE STATE PARK) The Forbay School was built in 1917 for the children of the employees of the Great Northern Power Company who lived in Forbay below the Thomson hydroelectric station. In 1931 the teacher had eight students and lived above the school. After the school closed in 1931, children attended the Lincoln School in Esko.

Forbay School, CCHS photo

WONGSTEDT (N-W-2-29-16) The school was built in 1887 on the St. Louis River Road. It burned 1918.

WASHINGTON SCHOOL (SE-SE-9-49-16)

During the years following the 1918 fires, school was held in the town hall, churches, and schools that had not burned. Following the fire, the new brick Washington school for grades 1-8 was built in 1919-20 two miles north of Esko on the North Road. In 1933 the district reorganized and Washington became the only elementary school in the township. Washington closed in 1980 and became a community center, which has now relocated to the new township hall.

Washington School, CCHS photo

ESKO COUNTRY SCHOOL (LINCOLN) THOMSON

(NW-NW-27-29-16) The first school in Esko was built in 1897 on the site of the future Lincoln School. This school escaped the 1918 fire. Later the old country school was moved from its schoolyard to its present location on highway 61, where it has been made into a museum by the Esko Historical Society.

LINCOLN SCHOOL THOMSON (NW-NW-27-29-16)

Lincoln School is located in section 27 on the current site of the Esko School and the original site of the old country school. It opened in the fall of 1920 with high school courses beginning that year. In 1933 it became a junior-senior high school. Additions were made in 1936 and 1955. In 1960 a new addition was made for the Winterquist Elementary School.

Lincoln School, CCHS photo

Esko eighth grade students, 1924, CCHS photo

27

DISTRICT 2
CARLTON SCHOOL (10-48-17)

Carlton is situated in Twin Lakes and Silverbrook Townships. Originally the village was called Northern Pacific Junction as the Northern Pacific Railroad yards were located there. On September 18, 1871, the village petitioned for a school district.

A typical frame building was built which had three teachers. It burned in 1895. A four-room school was built to replace it and it too burned in 1907. It was identical to the Barnum school, which also burned. This was an all too common event with large wood frame buildings, wood and coal furnaces, and no fire protection. They did have a metal chute on the side of the building, which acted as a fire escape. A two story red brick building was finally built in 1908. It was thought to be fireproof but lasted only seven years when it too went up in a spectacular blaze on February 16, 1915. The building had been fumigated following a scarlet fever epidemic and it was thought this was the cause of the fire, but it turned out to be bad wiring. Fires were so common it is a wonder that they did not hire someone to stand and watch over the furnace day and night. Students attended school in various public buildings until a new brick building was built on the same site in 1916 at a cost of $42,000. It remains on the same site with various additions and alterations.

The first graduating class was in 1910. In 1912 Carlton took in Thomson and consolidated small schools such as Iverson and Lone Pine. South Terrace was built in 1960 and the Sawyer School was closed.

The second Carlton School, built in 1895 to replace the first school, which had burned. This school also burned in a fire watched by many townspeople in 1907. CCHS photos

The new brick school was built in 1908 and it too burned on February 16, 1915. CCHS photos

Carlton School built in 1916 at a cost of $42,000.
CCHS photo

Carlton students, 1890s, CCHS photo

Carlton eighth grade class, 1923, CCHS photo

TWIN LAKES TOWNSHIP (48-16-15)

IVERSON SCHOOL (NW-NW-8-48-17)

Iverson was settled about 1900 by the Denser family and the school was open between about 1911 and 1931. Carlton took in Iverson in 1913. Former student Ruby Niemi said Maytie Beattie taught at the school the entire time it was open. After closing, the building was moved to Chubb Lake where it later burned.

LONE PINE (SW-SE-26-48-17)

Lone Pine seems to have operated between 1911 and 1933 and was located across from the Matten home on County Road 3. It was consolidated with Carlton in 1913.

Lone Pine School, near Scott's Corner, students and teacher in 1913-1914, CCHS photo

DISTRICT 2 - PLEASANT VIEW 1880s-1916 (NE-SW-6-47-17)

The school was built in the 1880s and was sold and moved in 1916 when it was replaced by the Blackhoof Valley School. It was referred to as the "pioneer school of Blackhoof Valley." It was located on County Highway 5 across from Hecker Road.

Pleasant View School students and teacher, 1907, CCHS photo

DISTRICT 3 - MOOSE LAKE SCHOOL (21-46-19)

The first school was organized March 11, 1873, with classes held in the railroad depot. The children were mostly Indian. In 1875, a school was built of rough boards by Swedish settlers. This may have been the site of Bethlehem Lutheran Church. Classes were also held in an old log building where the Red Owl was. It was replaced by the old frame town hall. In 1882 the first real school was built and was called the" little white school on the hill." *History of Moose Lake Volume 1* by Dave Anderson contains photos from 1883 and 1894. The building was later used for a church when the new school was built. In 1894 a large four-room two-story frame schoolhouse was built on the site of the village lot across from the power plant. Rev. Nilsen was superintendent of schools at the time. The first 8th grade graduation was held June 3, 1909. This school burned in the 1918 fire.

"The Little White School on the Hill" ca. 1894, photo Author's Collection

The 1894 two-story school, CCHS photo

A brick school was built in 1911 costing $55.000. It survived the 1918 fire and was used as a Red Cross station following the fire.

Ruins of Moose Lake following the 1918 forest fires. The brick Moose Lake School in the center of the photo was used as an emergency hospital after the fire. MLAHS photo by Levie

The first graduation class was in 1915 and had three students—Mildred Anderson, Lloyd Carlson, and Robert Mossberg. Rural students wanting four years of high school had to provide their own transportation. On January 25, 1935, the brick school burned. Following the fire, students were taught in every possible place including the jail. A new school was built and several additions were built later.

David Anderson's High School course completion certificate, 1909. MLAHS photo

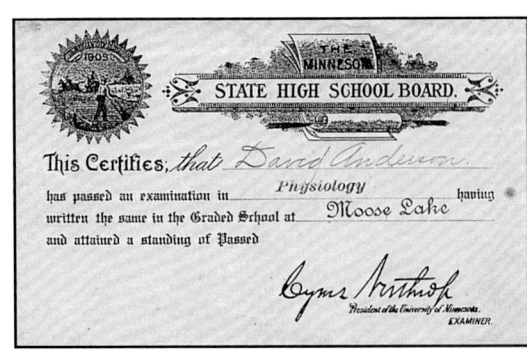

Moose Lake 8th grade graduation, l to r: Walter Johnson, David Anderson, Vernon Skelton, Fridolf Westholm, MLAHS photo

Boundary changes and consolidations followed after the fire. In 1936 the bus route extended to Split Rock and Beaver. In 1942 Lincoln, Birch Grove, and Eckman consolidated with Moose Lake. High School students from Kettle River, Split Rock, and Windemere joined. Moose Lake tried to get District 12 (Automba) but they thought 6 grades were enough for their children. Eight grades were barely tolerated. On September 6, 1957, Moose Lake became District 97. Schools continued to consolidate and boundaries changed. The Carlton County Historical Society would have these records as well as lists of teachers. In 1966 the people defeated a bond issue for a new school on a State Hospital site. In 1986 the district passed a bond issue for an elementary school and other additions. Elementary students remain in their own building and the high school is still in its old brick building, which has been remodeled and had several additions. In 1971, $400,00 was spent with more being allocated since then.

Original photographs and documents are on file at the Carlton County Historical Society and the Moose Lake Area Historical Society.

Sources: *1918 Fire Stories*
Fire Beast
History of Moose Lake Volume 1 by Dave Anderson
History of Moose Lake Volume II by Dave Anderson, 1989
Moose Lake, Kettle River and Surrounding Area, including the 1918 fire by Edwin Manni, 1968
The Other West Side Story

MOOSE LAKE HIGH SCHOOL WAS BURNED TO GROUND LAST FRIDAY

JANUARY 31, 1935

Special Writer Delves Into History of the Institution

Cause of Conflagration So Far Has Not Been Found

(By Mrs. C. F. Mahnke.)

With the village fire siren sounding the death knell to the continued life of the Moose Lake high school building Friday morning, many and varied were the reactions of those viewing the burning building. Many a social hour will be spent among those who were privileged, at one time or another, to tread its corridors, recalling the past-by saying, "Do you remember when—?" That fire erased many a tell-tale initial left upon its various surfaces throughout.

As gleanings from some of these "Do you remembers?" some interesting and important bits of information have been gathered.

It is brought out that about 1909, the population of our little community had increased to such an extent that the school attendance made it necessary to use the Swedish Lutheran church (site now occupied by the present high school) for housing the higher grades. The school board, consisting of Ole Swanson, John Lindmark, Fred Gay, S. A. Jacobson, N. G. Nilsen, and C. F. Mahnke, decided that something must be done in the way of better housing. School district No. 3 voted bonds to the state of Minnesota in the amount of $10,000 to be used for a new school building. The present site was chosen as much more favorable to build on than the old site. A 99-year lease was obtained from the village council to occupy a ten-acre tract of the village grounds near the lake as long as said grounds were used for school purposes.

The board secured the services of Clyde Kelly, an architect from Duluth to draw up plans and specifications. After a great deal of deliberation, the contract was finally let to L. J. Klippen, also of Duluth.

It was [illegible] the ground was first broken for this new building, C. F. Mahnke of this place turning the first shovel of ground. Every effort was put forth to have the building ready for occupancy in

(Turn to page 2, please.)

Cause of Conflagration So Far Has Not Been Found

(PHOTO PAGE 3.)

Fire, of unknown origin, completely destroyed Moose Lake's high school building and contents early last Friday morning. The alarm was turned in at around 3:00 a.m., but before the fire department arrived, it could be plainly seen that the building was doomed. However, the firemen worked valiantly until morning, trying to save the gymnasium, but they were powerless.

From an investigation it appeared the fire started on the first floor in the east wall of the building, but from an undetermined cause. It might have been from an overheated boiler, but this is doubtful; it may have been from defective wiring, or any one of many other causes. However, it was seen that the east side of the building was in flames, and the fire gradually ate its way through the structure until it was consumed. Of the contents, nothing was saved but two electric stoves from the domestic science department.

School in all probability, will resume a week from Monday, after new equipment, books, etc., arrive. Moose Lake's several churches will be used, as well as the Masonic temple and town hall. Sup't. R. J. Teska will have his office in the temple and this building will be used as a headquarters, it was said.

The board members have held several meetings since the fire, and have made a trip to Minneapolis, at which time necessary supplies were ordered. At the present time the matter of insurance is being adjusted.

Nothing has yet been done toward tearing down the walls of the old school, although it is expected this work will start shortly. Relief labor will be used.

While nothing definite has yet been done toward the erection of a new school, board members are doing all they can to speed this work. It is planned, according to one member, to build a new and modern structure, one up to the minute in every respect, with ample room for the future growth of the community.

Article about the Moose Lake School fire on January 25, 1935.

The burned out school.

The General Science class held at the Depot after the fire.
photos MLAHS

After the 1935 fire, classes were held in Masonic Temple (pictured at left), Zion Lutheran Church, the Methodist Church, the Northern Pacific Depot, the Village Hall, and even the jail.
MLAHS photo

The new school built after the fire, which is still in use.
CCHS photo

Mrs. Maki's 3rd and 4th grades, 1950-51, MLAHS photo

DISTRICT 4 - SANDY LAKE SCHOOL (SW-SE-19-47-17)

Sandy Lake district was organized in 1874. The school was 3 1/2 miles south of the Pleasant View School and one mile south of the Baptist Church. Al Naslund, boyhood resident of Sandy Lake community, said the school closed in 1941. Students then went to Central. Edna Hecker taught there until she died in 1927 and Carl Anderson took over.

PLEASANT VIEW SCHOOL (NE-SW-6-47-17)

In a published speech, Ernest Nelson stated it was the first school in the Blackhoof Valley and was known as the "pioneer school" of Blackhoof. It was replaced by the Blackhoof Valley School in 1916. See District # 36. Source: Florence Carlson

Sandy Lake School photo copy Author's Collection

DISTRICT 5 - MAHTOWA SCHOOL (NW-NE-9-47-18)

The district was established on October 25, 1875, and the first school was built. In 1885 a one-room school was established across the railroad tracks in a building that had housed a saloon. It was called "the little white school among the willows." Willie Newman, a local printer, built a model of the school, which is on display at the Carlton County Fair. Willie published a little newspaper using hand carved woodcuts, some of which featured students and the school. In 1904 a two-room frame school was built next to Salem Lutheran Church.

Recess at "the little white school" ca. 1900
CCHS photo

This school was the same style as the Park Lake School. A brick school was then built and used until replaced by a new school built in 1963. Mahtowa consolidated with Barnum and housed the elementary grades until the building was sold to a mortuary about 1988.

Sources: John Thompson, Claire Spoolman, Harold Olsen, Ron Osborne, Dorothy Radmacher, Florence Carlson, and Art Wallitalo. Also Mary Brett in Hjalmar Swanson's *History of Mahtowa*.

Mahtowa students and teachers in front of the school, May 16, 1913, photo by Oscar Lycander, courtesy of John M. U. Thompson

Mahtowa graduating class of 1913, CCHS photo

The brick Mahtowa School, June, 1963, CCHS photo

SCHOOL JOURNAL

MAHTOWA, MINN. • • • MARCH 20, 1899.

- LOCALS -

Mrs. W. Buttrick and daughter Gladys went to Grantsburg last week to attend the funeral of their cousin.

The northbound Limited last Sunday was about three hours late on account of the snow storm.

Mr. Rand has finished hauling Ole Bergs logs and has started cutting some more green timber near Kettle River.

Mrs. C. LeMay was visiting in Carlton last week.

Do not forget the Farmers Convention at Barnum the 23rd and 24th.

Ada Swenson accompanied her mother on a visit to St. Paul.

Johnnie Brett went to Barnum last Wednesday on business.

Atwood Lbr. Co. expect to finish logging the latter part of this week.

Mr. Rookey of Willow River, who is hauling logs into Mahtowa for Mr. Rand, had a valuable horse die last week.

Mr. Pat Brett came home from the woods Wednesday. We are glad to see our boys come back.

Men are very scarce around Mahtowa, some say girls are too -- ask Swan Anderson.

Election day passed off very quietly. The same officers were elected with the exeption of A. Swenson, Treasurer. Chas. Thompson was elected in his place.

The storms are 'Marching' along in regular order.

Several of our towns people are the recipients of invitations to the Grand Maccabees Ball to be held at Carlton.

The people of Mahtowa have finished harvesting a splendid crop of Park Lake ice.

Mahtowa School Journal, March 20, 1899, by Willie Newman, Author's Collection

Mahtowa School souvenir card, 1912
Author's Collection

Mahtowa students, ca. 1910-12,
photo Author's Collection

The first through fourth grades of Mahtowa School, 1939, photo courtesy of Earl Erickson

DISTRICT 6 - BARNUM SCHOOL (NW-NE-1-46-19)

The district was organized on March 1, 1880. The first school was the "white school" built at the top of the hill in 1885. In the 1890s a two-story red frame building was constructed next door. It was the same plan as the

The second Barnum school and students in 1904 with the first "white school" on the hill in the background, CCHS photo

school in Carlton and it too burned down. In 1908 Barnum became the 2nd consolidated school, with the addition of Anderson, Skelton, and Lind schools. In 1911 a new brick school was built. The brick school had just been enlarged to house high school classes when it burned on January 1, 1922. It was rebuilt and became a fully accredited four-year high school in 1923. A new library addition was built in 1928 and George G. Barnum donated two thousand books.

Horse drawn school buses, students, and dogs in front of the brick school, which was built in 1911. It was enlarged in 1921 and burned on January 1, 1922. CCHS photo

The third Barnum school
burned on January 1, 1922
and was quickly rebuilt.
CCHS photos

Barnum graduating class of 1943, CCHS photo

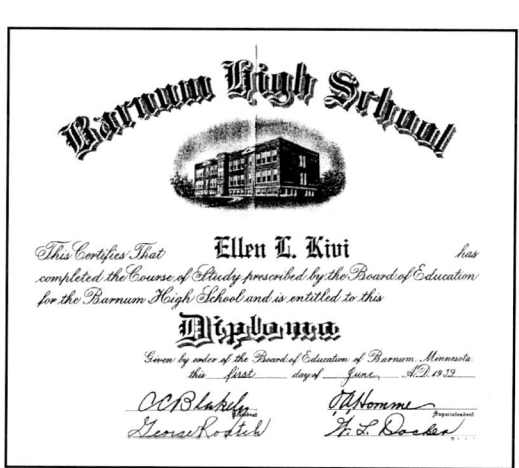

Barnum graduating class of 1903.
Front row, l to r: Clara Hecker,
Mr. Brophy, principal,
Louise Kreiger, Loraine Bolton
Standing: Pearl Skelton, Mayme Lee,
Luella Goodell, Ray Addington,
Minnie Siemer, Hannah Johnson
CCHS photo by Octavie Morneau

Miss Philips' first grade class at Barnum
CCHS photo

Paul Dathe at the blackboard
CCHS photo

BARNUM, CARLTON COUNTY, MINNESOTA, FRIDAY, FEBRUARY 8, 1918

LIMITED KILLS SEVEN CHILDREN

Badly Injuring Six Others Who Were Returning From School in Bus Last Friday Afternoon Driver Karl Miller Put Under Bonds and Held to District Court

Last Friday afternoon the Southbound Limited struck one of the school busses at the crossing near the depot in which 24 children were returning to their homes from school and hurled it to one side instantly killing six of the children and injuring another so that it [died] before a physician could attend it although it was rushed to Willow River for medical attention. Others injured were taken to the hospital at Moose Lake where all but four returned the next day to their homes near here. Those who were killed were:

WILLIAM FOGARTY, age 15,
HOMER STOLLER, age 16,
JOHN H. KAIVO, age 12,
CHARLES H. KAIVO, age 7,
ARTHUR W. KAIVO, age 6,
ALTHA HARRINGTON, age 14,
MARY SNOECKS, age 15.

The injured were Marian Fogarty, seriously about head; John Gowan, leg broken and other injuries; Gilbert Jarvis, Gladys McCandless, Harold Hagen and Warren Doan. Of these the four last have been removed from the hospital to their homes and John Gowan has been taken to St. Mary's hospital and Marian Fogarty still remains and is said to be in a comatose state but is said to be improving.

Other children who were in the bus at the time and who escaped injury were: Florence Duesler, Florence Beck, Lilly Christensen, Alice Doan, Vera Crook, Lempi Kaivo, Ella Harrington, Della Dutry, Fred Doan, Fred Gowan and Charlie Hall.

It appears from the evidence given at the inquest that the [driver]

while passing this place and as his train was about nine minuets late he was trying to regain the time lost and was running about 40 or 42 miles an hour. The jury composed of Messrs. Oscar Anderson, A. H. Dathe, H. R. Patterson, C. L. Goodell, John Medo and H. Gerlach brought in a verdict charging the driver with culpable negligence. Mr. Miller was taken to Carlton and held till yesterday when he was examined before Justice Frees and held in $1,000 bonds to the next term of the district court. The bonds were furnished by Thos. Spencer and W. M. Hogan.

The body of Mary Snoecks was taken to Superior Saturday night by her father who came down from the city to take it with him for burial.

The funeral of Homer Stoller was held Monday morning from the M. E. church where a large number of the boy's friends had assembled to do him the last honor they were able. A large number of them were unable to gain [entrance to the little church]

George G. Barnum 1918, Minnesota Historical Society photo by Lee Brothers

Above: Article from the *Barnum Herald* about a tragic school bus-train accident, February 8, 1918

In 1922 George G. Barnum made a donation to purchase books for the new Barnum school library.

GEORGE G. BARNUM
DULUTH, MINN. Oct. 31st '22

Miss Florence Naseem Sec.

Dear Miss Naseem

Thanks for your letter, in which (speaking for your class) you tell me how you expended your share of the donation I gave the School, I should say you made good use of it in your selection, Now if you make good use of the Books, and absorb their contents, I shall feel glad, I was able to add to your knowledge & happiness,

note you have started a Literary Society & have named it after me, I am sending the Society some of the World's best literature & if there is anything you especially need in this line of endeavor, let me know, I sent you my picture the other day than you asked for,

The children of today are to be the rulers of the World later, to be well governed it is necessary to be well educated, so I hope you will take all the advantages that come your way & fit yourselves to be the leaders of tomorrow, please convey to your class my appreciation of their action in naming your Society after me

Your sincerely

Geo. G. Barnum

HISTORICAL OUTLINE OF CLOQUET SCHOOLS___🖉

1881 **School District #7 organized January 4, 1881**, with W. T. David as the only teacher

1883 (or 1884?)   First two-room wood frame school house built.

1890 Two new schools added: Washington School (brick) built on Avenue C in the west end (Washington School was later known as Central School) and Jefferson School, a wood-frame building, built on Cloquet Avenue between 8th & 9th Streets. The first high school classes held in Washington School, teachers' wages at this time $45-$50 a month until about 1902.

1894 School Board enters into agreement with the government to teach Indian children, $1/pupil/year.

1895 School enrollment 500 students and 12 teachers.

1897 Cloquet graduates its first two students—Helen Johnson and Agnes Forslund. Graduation ceremonies held at the Opera House with admission of fifteen cents.

1898 A new brick Jefferson School (eight rooms) built and the wood frame building moved to 6th Street and Carlton Avenue. It became Lincoln School.

1899 No Cloquet High School graduating class. First truant officer hired.

1900 August 18 (*Pine Knot*) all school buildings officially named by School Board.

1901 Horse-drawn wagons serve as buses for students living north of the river. Four rooms added to Lincoln School.

1902 Scarlet fever epidemic closes school from February 21 until March 24. W. Cobb is the superintendent.

1904 Cloquet becomes a city. First music teacher hired by school.

1905 A new ten-room high school built on Carlton Avenue at the cost of $35,000. The old building (then named Lincoln) moved down to 14th Street and becomes Garfield.

1907 Twenty Cloquet High School students graduate.

1909 Garfield School completed at a cost of $25,000. Fifteen cents charged for graduation. Old Garfield moved south one lot.

1910 Peter Olesen hired as superintendent. Thirty-seven teachers paid $65/month. Commercial teacher hired.

1912 The Parochial School started. Showers added to Cloquet high school.

1914 The Cloquet Junior College formed and lasts until 1923. School nurse hired after smallpox outbreak.

1915 Night school classes started for foreign-born residents who want to learn English

1917 World War I starts, Ralph Gellerman is the first Cloquet H.S. senior to enlist. His brother Milo is the second. Thirty-eight graduate. Ramsey Smith gets horse-drawn wagon contract to transport children on Reservation Road.

1918 In April a new high school built at the cost of $100,000. After the great fire on October 12, Garfield School is the only school left standing and becomes a hospital and Red Cross Center until December 9 when classes start up again.

1919 Building begins on a new High School. It opens in 1921. Leach School added to the district at a cost of $63,000.

1926 Motorized school buses first used.

1936 Garfield adds new classrooms.

1938 An addition built at the High School including a gymnasium. Garfield School also added onto and refaced.

1948 Gymnasiums added to Garfield and Leach Schools.

1952 Addition built at the High School.

1956 Washington School built on 12th Street and Doddridge Avenue.

1957 Leach School adds new classrooms.

1958 New wing added to the High School, and an indoor pool built.

1962 Churchill School built. W. Gessner hired as superintendent.

1967 Present High School built on 18th Street. Opens in 1968.

1969 Jefferson School closed.

1975 Lincoln School closed.

1978 Leach School closed.

1981 New auto shop opens at Senior High School. Garfield closes as Elementary School and is now a Community Center.

1987 Athletic complex completed at Senior High School.

1988 Early Childhood Special Education addition completed at Churchill Elementary School.

1992 Major additions completed at Washington and Churchill Elementary Schools.

1994 Excess levy referendum passes for implementation of District Technology Plan.

Cloquet is the largest city in Carlton County and the history of Cloquet schools can be found in a number of previously published volumes. This abbreviated outline of Cloquet school history is adapted from *Cloquet High School Centennial Memory Book 1897 - 1997* and is used with permission of the Cloquet Educational Foundation. Additional Cloquet school history is available at the Carlton County Historical Society.

Washington School students, Cloquet, ca. 1890s, CCHS photo

Washington School, later known as Central, built 1890. CCHS photo

Cloquet High School, built in 1905

First Cloquet High School graduates—
Helen Johnson and Agnes Forslund, 1897

Early Cloquet teachers, ca. 1898

Above right: the second Cloquet High
School, built in early in 1918 and destroyed
in the forest fire on October 12, 1918
Ruins photo by Olaf Olson

The third Cloquet High School opened
in 1921 and is now the site of Cloquet
Middle School.

CCHS photos

Old Garfield School

Garfield School was the only school remaining after the 1918 fire and was used as a hospital and Red Cross Center. When classes resumed in December, two shifts were held to accommodate all of the Cloquet students.

Leach Kindergarten Band, 1934
photo by Olaf Olson

Jefferson Junior High School, ca. 1940s

CCHS photos

The fourth Cloquet High School, built in 1967-68 on 18th Street

DISTRICT 8 - NEMADJI /CENTRAL SCHOOL 1912-1963
(NE-NE-3-46-18)

District 8 was formed March 15, 1881. It was the first rural consolidated school district in Minnesota. Consolidation was done in September of 1912 and was made up of three schools: Connor, District 8; Bennie Peterson, District 29; and Huffman's Corner, District 23. Special legislation was required to do this and to build a teacherage, which was later moved to the Ted Paulson property in Barnum.

In early years, high school was not available unless one was able to procure transportation. In 1912-1921, Central had grades 1-10; in 1921-22, two years of high school; and in 26-27, four years of high school. In 1928 grades 1-8 combined with Barnum High School. In 1951 Central consolidated with Barnum, to become part of District 6. Central became a K-6 school. Central closed in 1963 and students attended a brand new elementary school in Barnum.

Central School opened in 1912. CCHS photo

The old Central was torn down in 1963 after 51 years of service. Former students have a great sentimental attachment and hold a reunion every summer during county fair week.

Teachers: Uola Gulliford Hecker, May Nelson Froberg. Louise Swenson County Superintendent of Schools, 1940.

Central School Grades 3, 4, 5, 1950-51, teacher Emma Bell. MLAHS photo by P. Schawang

CONNOR SCHOOL (8) (SE-SE-32-47-18)

Built between Central and Barnum as early as 1881. It was one of the three schools that were the first consolidated schools in the State of Minnesota. It was located on County 6 and Maple Drive.

Connor School and students 1908, CCHS photo

HUFFMAN'S CORNERS also called FELGIN'S (8) (23) 1899-1912 (SE-SE-15-46-18)

Huffman's Corners was located a mile south of the village of Nemadji near the intersection of Mud Creek Road and County Road 11. It was one of three schools that consolidated to form Nemadji Central School in 1912.

BENNY PETERSON (8) 1903-1912 (Section 1 or 2-46-18)

Consolidated with Central, Huffman's Corner, and Connor in 1912. It was located on Co. Roads 6 and 11 (Deer Park Road) approximately one mile east of Central School site. After the school closed it was moved across Deer Park Road and used as a home.

Sources: Carl Anderson, Howard Ballou, Olive Ballou, Mary Ballou, Lester Duesler. Gordy Schwoch

A student remembers...
" All the students from 1-8 were our friends. Many times a young student doing seat work would be listening to the older classes. I'm sure a lot of that information was retained and brought to mind when we reached that grade."

DISTRICT 9 - WRENSHALL (Pleasant Valley)
McKINLEY SCHOOL (NW-NW-5-47-16)

District 9 was organized December 13, 1884, A *Pine Knot* article from 1977 says the school was moved in 1902 or '03 to the site shown on 1914 and later maps and that it was sold in 1905. Since a school census from 1931 and a list of teachers from 1933-34 exist, there is a question as to just what years school was actually held at McKinley. W.W. Kirkpatrick was a Principal. Dissolved and annexed to #15 August 3, 1937.

McKinley School students, ND, CCHS photo

McKinley School Census, 1931

McKinley School, Wrenshall, early 1900s
CCHS photo

SCHOOL CENSUS (To be made between July 1st and October 1st.)

The following is a complete School Census of all children between six (6) and sixteen (16) years of age residing in School District No. 9 in Carlton County, Minnesota, Dated Sept 30 1931.

McKinley school

NAME	Month	Day	Year	Age	Name of Parent or Guardian	POST OFFICE
Anderson, Myrtle	Feb.	23	1920	11	Wm Anderson	Wrenshall
" Lillian	Jan.	3	1922	9	"	"
" Isabelle	Nov.	8	1924	6	"	"
Goad, Harold	Feb.	4	1918	13	G. E. Goad	Wrenshall
" Everett	Dec.	26	1922	9	"	"
Haubner, Robert	Oct.	21	1918	13	Jack Haubner	Wrenshall
Hammill, Gearold	Nov.	6	1916	15	Fred Hammill	
" Leva	Nov.	20	1924	7		
Mattson, Edna	Apr.	23	1919	12	Andrew Mattson	Wrenshall
" David	Feb.	21	1921	10	"	
" Oscar	Sept.	5	1923	8	"	
Eng, Merton	Dec.	17	1925	5	Arthur Eng	Wrenshall
" Melvin	Dec.	17	1925	5	"	
Palmer, John	Nov.	16	1920	11	Floyd Palmer	
" Laura	Jan.	21	1922	9	"	"
" Caroline	Jan.	2	1923	8	"	"
" George	June	12	1924	7	"	"
" Lawrance	Aug	3	1925	5	"	"
Payne, Irene	Nov.	14	1922	9		
" James	Feb.	23	1924	7		
Stewart, Martha Lou	Mar.	19	1924	7	G. A. Stewart	
Storey, Warren	Aug	4	1921	10	Anna Storey	
" Richard	Feb.	18	1923	8	"	
Wanquist, Raymond	Dec.	7	1919	12	Walter Wanquist	
" Donald	May	15	1921	10	"	
" Alfan	Dec.	17	1923	8	"	"
Byrnes, Alice	Jan.	23	1918	13	Elery Hoyle	
" Lynell	June	3	1921	10	"	
Paulson, Lucille	Aug.	25	1920	11	L. C. Paulson	
Vielleux, Clinton	June	14	1925	6	Mario Vielleux	

Students remember...

"By the time you walked two miles and milked cows before you left home, you were tired and happy to sit where it was warm."

"I finished the 8th grade and didn't attend after that. My dad died and I had to become a man (at 14 years) and help mother and my little sister."

DISTRICT 10 - GUNDERSON 1905-1940 (NE-NW-32-46-18)

The district was organized July 8, 1885. According to Dave Anderson's book, this school was built on the site of Eddy Maygren's home in 1905. In 1915 it was moved to the Gunderson farm and later enlarged to accommodate increased attendance. It operated until 1940 and the building was later used by the Assemblies of God church before they built. The district officially? consolidated with Moose Lake in 1950.

Source: Evelyn and Clarence Sway

Gunderson School, 1914, MLAHS photo

Gunderson students, 1912-13
1st row left: Ethel Larson, Martha Johnson, Carrie Gustafson, Edna Gunderson, 2nd row: Mattie Jordet, Mabel Larson, Karen Jordet, Julia Jordet, 3rd row: Hartley Gunderson, Redmond Brink, Mauritz Johnson, Eleanor Johnson, Maulins Brink, Engval Folstad
Teacher: Laura Goman
Standing: Clara Johnson, Alma Larson, Florence Larson, Ray Gunderson.
photo Author's Collection

MUD CREEK (NW-SE-24-46-19)

The school was built along the Military Road in 1893. First classes were held in a log house south of the Chris Moser and Kahrings farms. Some early teachers were Ernst Rohlf, Eddie Fisher, Agnes Granfield, Mary Doyle, Mabel Waldron, and Minnie Siemer. The school closed in 1943 and was sold to Moose Lake Implement where the building remains.

Rose Kahring in front of the
Mud Creek School,
ca. early 1900s, MLAHS photo

Mud Creek School
District No. 10
Barnum Township,
Carlton County, Minn.
→ 1909-10 ←

MINNIE E. SIEMER, Teacher

Pupils

Lydia Aldrin	Samuel Aldrin
Clara Borg	Mabel Barquist
Howard Belford	Minnie Carlson
Walter Carlson	Jerome Duquette
Mary Flaa	Alice Flaa
Jennie Hagstrom	Minnie Hanson
Etta Hass	Fred Kahring
Martha Kahring	Tony Moser
Allie Moser	Bertha Moser
Julia Moser	Frank Moser
Reuben Matson	Lawrence Matson
Alice Matson	Hilton Norman
Manley Norman	Myrtle Norman
Clarence Nyberg	Arthur Nyberg
Eddie Peterson	John Holden
Herbert Holden	Alfred Sieverson
Signe Sieverson	Mary Sieverson
Harvey Wiberg	Ephriam Wiberg

SCHOOL OFFICERS
C. Moser, Director   J. Kahring, Clerk
A. Gunderson, Treasurer
J. E. Colovin, County Superintendent

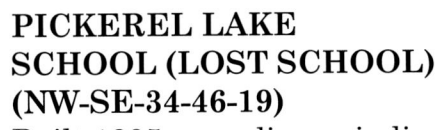

Mud Creek Christmas program, 1934
MLAHS photo

PICKEREL LAKE SCHOOL (LOST SCHOOL) (NW-SE-34-46-19)

Built 1905 or earlier as indicated by a dated photograph. This school was called the "Lost School" as the builder, William Abbott, could not locate the site. It burned in the 1918 fire and was not rebuilt.

Pickerel Lake School (Lost School),
1915, MLAHS photo

DISTRICT 11 - WRIGHT SCHOOL (NE-NE-4-48-41)

The district was organized November 13, 1886, and a log structure served as the first school. A one-room frame building was later built. Then in 1908 a two-story brick building was built north of the railroad tracks and slightly west of the Lincoln school site. In 1928 there were students in grades 1-9. In 1940 a new brick school was built and the old school was turned into a gym after part of the upper story was removed. In 1965 Wright became an elementary school (Lincoln) with older children going to Cromwell. From 1952-64, Wright and Eagle were both elementary schools for Cromwell Schools. All students began going to a new school in Cromwell in 1993 and the Wright School was closed.

Consolidations: Nilsen (Brennick), Central, Norton, and Lakeside.

Wright school children and teachers, ca. 1910s
CCHS photo

Wright School, built in 1908
photo copy Author's Collection

Wright Rhythm Band, 1932-33, CCHS photo

Lincoln School, Wright
photo copy Author's Collection

A Student Remembers...

"I remember beginning our day with each one standing up and reciting the Pledge of Allegiance—that was a 'must'."

DISTRICT 12 - AUTOMBA TOWNSHIP (25 & 37)
1888-1906 (NW-NE-32-47-21)

District 12 was organized on September 20, 1888. Originally school was held in a pool hall or hotel. It is unclear whether an actual school building existed before the 1918 fire, although some sources indicate there was a building that burned in the fire. After the fire, school was held in the Kerttu house and later in a house built by Charlie Jokimaki. The Matt Reed house was also used. A new school was built in 1922 (24?) and consolidated in 1924 with Erickson and Karlson. They did not choose to consolidate with Kalevala in 1929. In 1937 the school was down to 19 students. Grades 1-8 went to Kalevala and high school students went to Barnum and Cromwell. In 1970 the district dissolved. The school became a cheese factory and later burned or was torn down.

BJORKLUND 1908 or earlier-1929
(NW-NE-26-47-21)

The school burned in the 1918 fire, was rebuilt, and consolidated with Kalevala in 1929.

JOKIMAKI 1906-1929
(NE-NW-14-47-21)

The school burned in the 1918 fire, was rebuilt in 1919, and consolidated in 1929 into Kalevala. The building was reused as a granary on a farm.

Bjorklund School, ND, photo Author's Collection

ERICKSON Dates uncertain (NE-NE-8-47-21)

The school burned in 1918 and was rebuilt. Consolidated with Automba in 1924.

Michaelson building as Sacred Heart Catholic Church
photo Author's Collection

MICHAELSON 1897-mid 1920s
(SE-SE-19-46-20)

The school was named after John Michaelson, who was one of the first trustees of the district, along with Frank Eckman and Thomas Ronkainen. This school probably burned in 1908 and was later re-built. The building was then used as Sacred Heart National (Polish) Catholic Church.

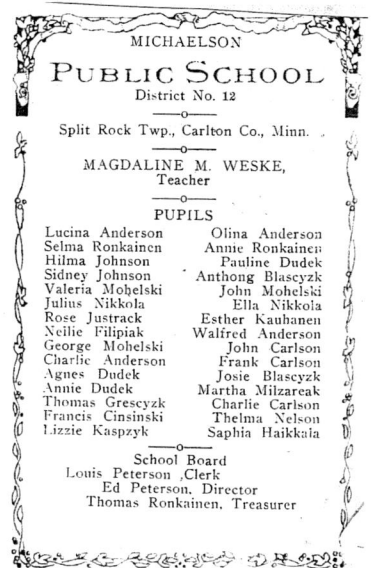

MICHAELSON
PUBLIC SCHOOL
District No. 12

Split Rock Twp., Carlton Co., Minn.

MAGDALINE M. WESKE,
Teacher

PUPILS

Lucina Anderson — Olina Anderson
Selma Ronkainen — Annie Ronkainen
Hilma Johnson — Pauline Dudek
Sidney Johnson — Anthong Blascyzk
Valeria Mohelski — John Mohelski
Julius Nikkola — Ella Nikkola
Rose Justrack — Esther Kauhanen
Neilie Filipiak — Walfred Anderson
George Mohelski — John Carlson
Charlie Anderson — Frank Carlson
Agnes Dudek — Josie Blascyzk
Annie Dudek — Martha Milzareak
Thomas Grescyzk — Charlie Carlson
Francis Cinsinski — Thelma Nelson
Lizzie Kaspzyk — Saphia Haikkala

School Board
Louis Peterson ,Clerk
Ed Peterson, Director
Thomas Ronkainen, Treasurer

KARLSON 1901/2-1924 (SE-SW-21-47-21)

It was located 1/2 mile west of County Highway 6 on Kahara Road prior to the 1918 fire. The school burned in 1918, was rebuilt, and consolidated with Automba in 1924.

Karlson students prior to 1918 fire.
l to r, back row: Waino Mattson, Hanna Johnson, Wendla Nynas, Lempi Korhonen, Anna Johnson. front row: Arvi Mattson (died in the 1918 fire), Arvo Mattson, Hugo Hendrickson, Charley Mattson, Jenny Maijala.
CCHS photo

ECKMAN 1891-1936 (SE-NW-23-46-20)

The first school west of town in District 12 was conducted in one of two rooms of a log house built by John R. Johnson. It was used until 1890, when a school was built on the north side of the "West Road" near the Charles Eckman farm home. School began there in January 1891. The first teachers were Willie Gray, Jennie Stone, Etta Miller, Flora Brown, and Maggie Swanson. Among the first students were Gust Olson, Eddie Peterson, Esther Peterson, William Haney, Ed Westerberg, and Ludwig Olson. An addition was built in 1904, making it a two-room school with

Eckman School, teachers, and students, 1908, MLAHS photo

two teachers. For the first few years there were only four or five months of school. Annie Carlson and her cousin Ella Carlson were the first 8th grade graduates to go on to a higher institution of learning, enrolling at the Duluth Normal School. Later on Annie Carlson taught in the upper four grades of the Eckman School for two years. Anna Fossom taught the other four lower grades.This school was also used on Sunday for religious services whenever some visiting pastor was available. Sunday school was held in the afternoon with Mr. Eckman, Mr. Peterson, and Charlie Carlson as teachers.The school burned in the 1918 fire and was rebuilt. Eckman closed after consolidation with Moose Lake in 1936.

**BIRCH GROVE/
SANDBLOM/
1908/9-1934
(SE-NW-34-46-20)**
The Birch Grove (Sandblom) School was built to accommodate the area southwest of the Eckman School. The Sandblom family bought the school building in 1918 for part of their home

Birch Grove School
photo Author's Collection

and a new larger school was built in the same area. The new school survived the 1918 fire and was a refuge for those affected by the fire. Lower grades attended Birch Grove and upper grades Eckman school. It consolidated with Moose Lake in 1934 and the building was dismantled.

Birch Grove Play Day, 1932
photo Author's Collection

SCHOOL DISTRICT 13

CROMWELL TOWNSHIP (NW-NE-4-48-20)

District 13 was organized June 17, 1891, and a school was built on one half acre of land given by George Wright, Sr. Barbara Eher of Moose Lake was the first teacher and there were six students: Lydia and Daisy Paine, Jerry and Minnie Bellanger, and Erwin Newton and his sister. The Little Green School was the first school. It was spared when the Hinckley Fire roared through on September 1, 1894, but later it burned in June of 1900.

A second school was built of brick in 1900 and had an enrollment of about 40 pupils. A new school was being built in 1912. The older school burned about January 1, 1913, and school was held temporarily in the Morse store and some warehouses by the lake. The new school, designed by Duluth architect Clyde Kelly, was completed in 1913 and it was a grade school until the 1920s when a high school was added. It remained as a part of Cromwell school until the 1990s. Additions to the school were made in 1939, 1964, and 1976. By 1952, grades 1-6 were at

Cromwell School, 1905, CCHS photo by Smith Studio

Eagle Lake and Wright. By 1964 all grade school children went to Wright. A new school was built in the 1990s after which all grades began going to Cromwell in 1993.

Beck, Bennet A., *Brief History of the Pioneers of the Cromwell, Minnesota Area*, Carlton County Historical Society, 2001 Cromwell Reunion book

The "new" Cromwell School, ND, CCI IS photo

Cromwell School
Grades 3 and 4, 1925
CCHS photo

BECK SCHOOL (NW-NW-15-48-20—probably)

The school was in the vicinity of Robert Beck's residence on SW shore of Island Lake near Cromwell and named after him. School dates are unknown.

RED CLOVER TOWNSHIP:

SWANSON SCHOOL (NW-NW-12-49-2 0)

The school existed prior to 1914 and after 1927. Cromwell reunion book says that it "was located up Jonas Heikkila's way."

ASHLEY SCHOOL (SE-SE-5-49-20)

Ashley was one of first one-room rural schools in the district. It closed in 1928 and students were bussed to Cromwell.
Source: Ed Johnson

WALKER SCHOOL (SE-SW-26-49-20)

The Cromwell reunion book says this school was in operation only two years and was located near the Frank Hanson property.

Cromwell district school bus #1, ca. 1938. photo copy Author's Collection

DISTRICT 14 SAWYER SCHOOL (SW-NE or SE-NW-4-48-18)

The district was organized January 30, 1893. A school was built in 1902, which was open to whites on the reservation. The school burned in 1904 and was rebuilt in 1905 for grades 1-6. In 1922 a new school was built. It was located north of Highway 210 and used 1922-1960. It replaced a school that was located in Sawyer south of the tracks on a hill. Elaine Olson recounts that on the opening day of the new Sawyer School in 1922 all of the students gathered at the old school and walked in a line to the new school to the north. Older students went to Carlton. The school was abandoned when South Terrace grade school was built in Carlton.

Ruins of the Sawyer School, 2002, CCHS photo by Marlene Wisuri

PARK LAKE Early 1890s-1944 (SE-SW-29-48-18)

The first school at Park Lake was held in the early 1890s in an upstairs room in John Swenson's house. The next year a school was built close to Park Lake on what was later a picnic grounds belonging to Salem Lutheran Church. Around 1904 a two-room school was built a few hundred feet south of the lake. After the school closed in 1944, the building was sold to the Covenant Bible Camp and is still in use. Students were bussed to Barnum after the closing of the school.

Park Lake School, 1912, CCHS photo

Park Lake students, 1903, CCHS photo

The former Park Lake School, now part of the Covenant Church camp, CCCHS photo

Souvenir

1905

PARK LAKE
PUBLIC SCHOOL
District No. 14

Atkinson Twp., Carlton Co., Minn.

EDITH L. JOHNSON, Teacher

Pupils

John Asproth	Anton Bengston
Anton Carlson	Arthur Carlson
Nels Christensen	Sena Christensen
Herbert Christensen	Emil Christensen
Otto Christensen	Emma Danielson
Ingabor Danielson	Edward Eyberg
Minnie Eyberg	Elizabeth Fitzsimmons
Everett Fitzsimmons	
Matthew Fitzsimmons	
Jacob Gram	Arvid Lindberg
Phebe Lindberg	Eleonora Lundberg
Lillian Lundberg	Mabel Lundberg
Ruth Lundsten	Margarete Lundsten
Anton Lindquist	Clarence Nelson
Elmer Nelson	Albert Peterson
Annie Peterson	Emma Peterson
Alfred Peterson	Walter Peterson

Dave Fitzsimmons - - Director
George Watson - - - Clerk
Andrew Blomquist - Treasurer

58

DISTRICT 15
WRENSHALL TOWNSHIP 1894-Present (NW-NW-28-48-16)

The district was organized on January 2, 1894 and annexed District 9 on August 3, 1937. The original school in 1884 was upstairs of a grocery. Ella Coryell was the first teacher. A two-room school was built later at the old Al Lundberg place. A four-room school was built at Meyers Corner with two grades in each room. In 1906 two rooms were added. At this time the school was called Lincoln and had 150 students. In 1922 the school was torn down and rebuilt. The 1937 annexation took in Pleasant View, Praefke, Holyoke, and Barker schools. In 1932-37 teachers made $30-50 dollars a month and paid $2-5 for board.

Teachers: Florence Peters, Helmi Antilla, Ina Kinnunen

Board members: Joel Wainio, Matt Reed, Frank Erickson, Axel Pietila, John Carlson, and Henry Karki.

Wrenshall students and teachers, ca. 1898
CCHS photo

Wrenshall (Lincoln), 1914, CCHS photo

Wrenshall 8th and 9th grade graduation class, 1914
Teacher and principal W. W. Kirkpatrick,
teacher Dorothy Scott, CCHS photo

Wrenshall School, 1923, CCHS photo

Wrenshall students, 1923, CCHS photo

PLEASANT VIEW 15 (NE-SW 6-47-17)
The school operated from 1889-1916. It was sold and moved in 1916 and the Blackhoof Valley School was built 1/2 mile to the south. Also referred to as the Pioneer School of Blackhoof Valley and was located on County Highway 5 across from Hecker Road.

PRAEFKE SCHOOL 15 (SW-SW-16-47-16)
The school may have replaced McKinley, which was sold in 1905. It closed in 1934. In 1982 the dilapidated Praefke School, which was being used for Wrenshall's town hall, was renovated to look like an old school to use for historic functions and re-created pioneer school programs. The building burned in the mid 1980s.

MCKINLEY SCHOOL 15 Dates uncertain (NW-NW-5-47-16)
See District #9.

BARKER SCHOOL 15 (SW-SW-1-47-16)
It was located on County Road 6. Possibly built in 1913 and closed in early 1930s.

DISTRICT 16 KALEVALA SCHOOL (SW-SW-20-47-20)

Kalevala district was organized July 30, 1894. A $50,000 brick school was built in 1929 as consolidated school district #16. It took in Mansikka, Hokkanen, Salo, Koster-Holmi, and Konsti. It had six teachers and 209 students in grades 1-8 with Helen Harmala as principal. After 8th grade, some students went on to high school in Cromwell, Moose Lake, or Barnum. The Kalevala School closed in 1969 and students were split between Barnum and Cromwell. On July 1, 1970 the district was dissolved. The building burned April 1, 1975.

Kalevala School, built 1929
MLAHS photo

Kalevala Band, 1933-34. Director
Dagmar Mietinen, CCHS photo

KALEVALA SCHOOL SONG
Kalevala, Kalevala
Dear old school of ours
We will always firmly stand
With our friends so true

Kalevala, Kalevala
Let our praises ring
Ring out from hearts that bring
Success to thee

Kalevala students on the last day of school, 1950 CCHS photo

Kalevala 1st and 2nd grades, 1947, teacher Mrs. McIntyre, CCHS photo

Arson suspected 4-30-1975

Kalevala School, famous landmark destroyed by flames Wed.

At about 6:45 Wednesday morning the Kalevala School was reported burning. The Kettle River, Moose Lake and Barnum Fire Departments responded. The fire was completely out of control and saving the structure was impossible. According to authorities, the rear door of the school appeared to have been "jimmied" and arson was suspected. Value of the loss was not obtainable at presstime.

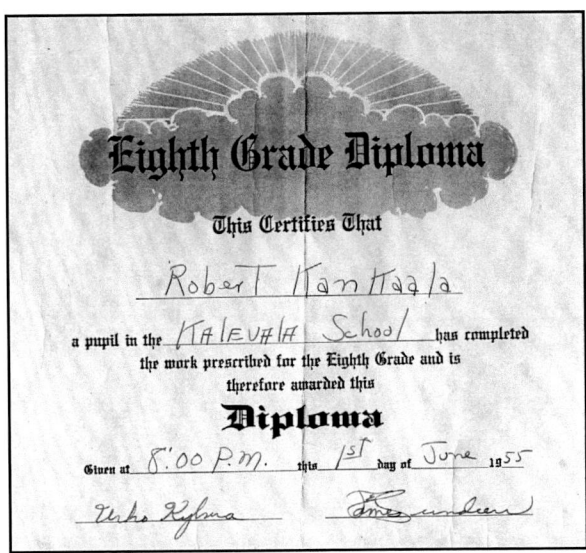

Eighth Grade Diploma

This Certifies That

Robert Kanttaala

a pupil in the Kalevala School has completed the work prescribed for the Eighth Grade and is therefore awarded this

Diploma

Given at 8:00 P.M. this 1st day of June 1955

Uno Kylma

A student remembers...

When I started school there were a few children who didn't speak English very well— mostly Finnish. Our school was mostly of Finnish ancestry—I'd say about 98%.

Mansikka students and their two teachers Lempi Rautio and Aune Martin, ca. 1923, photo Author's Collection

MANSIKKA SCHOOL #1 1895-1929 (SE-NE-30-47-20) at the SE corner of the A. Reed farm on Hwy 73

The original building was built by Mike Neimela in 1895 and survived 1918 fire. Another classroom was later built by Charles Jalonen in 1920. The first teacher was Ludwig Olson. The building was 1/2 mile east of the 1929 brick building. It consolidated with Kalevala in 1929. The building was torn down in 1931. Prior to the building of Mansikka, school was taught in the homes of Alex Mattson, Lambert Henrikson, and Joe Mansikka.

Before the school was razed in 1931, former students, the builder, and teacher gathered at Mansikka School, CCHS photo

SALO #2 also called RANUA (NE-SE-7-47-20)
The school was built in 1898 with an addition in 1907 on Hwy 73, 2 1/2 miles north of 14. Either the school did not burn or was rebuilt and was consolidated 1929.

Teachers: Lena Blaha Anderson, Mathiason, Ludwig Olson, 1909, Ella Sandstrom, Ella Rogers, Hortense Beaupre, Mildred Smith Little.

BJORKLUND #3 1898-1906 (NW-NE-26-47-21)
The school burned in 1918, was rebuilt, and consolidated in 1929. The building was used as a town hall until the late 1960s. See District # 12.

HOLMI-KOSTER (NASI) #4 1905-1916 (SE-SW-14-47-20)
The school was built in 1905. By 1916, the building was moved west to the Nasi farm. (NW-NE-22-47-20) It survived the 1918 fire and operated until 1923 when it was sold and the Hokkanen School was built to replace it.

HOKKANEN #4
1923-1929
(NE-NW-15-47-20)
The school was built in 1923 to replace Nasi and it was consolidated with Kalevala in 1929.

Hokkanen School, CCHS photo

Hokkanen School students
photo Author's Collection

NORDBERG/STENMAN #5
1906 or 08-1929
(NE-NE-4-46-20) one mile
north and 1/2 mile east of Kettle River on County Road 6.
The school was burned in 1918 and rebuilt in 1919 at a cost of $1,818. It consolidated in 1929 with Kalevala. The building was sold to Nick Nummela for $180 who sold it four years later to John Rudabeck.

I give this Nick Nummela the full privilege of the selling the school building.

Mrs. Sophia Stenman

Documents regarding the sale of the Stenman School
building, Author's Collection

B268—BILL OF SALE   A. M. OSWALD - Law Blanks - NEW ULM, MINN.

Know all Men by these Presents; That
Nick Numela

of the County of Carlton and State of Minnesota
party of the first part, in consideration of the sum of
One Dollar and other good and valuable consideration - - - - - - - DOLLARS,
to him in hand paid by John T. Rudabeck
of the County of Carlton and State of
Minnesota party of the second part, the receipt whereof is hereby acknowledged, do
hereby Grant, Bargain, Sell and Convey unto the said party of the second part, his executors, administrators and assigns, forever, the following described Goods, Chattels and Personal Property, to-wit:

One school building (known as Stenman School) located on the
Northeast Quarter of the Northeast Quarter (NE¼ of NE¼)
of Section Four (4), Township Forty-six (46), Range Twenty (20).

To Have and to Hold the Same, Unto the said party of the second part, his executors, administrators and assigns, Forever. And the said party of the first part, for himself, his heirs, executors and administrators, covenants and agrees to and with the said party of the second part, his executors, administrators and assigns, to Warrant and Defend the Sale of said Goods, Chattels and Personal Property hereby made, unto the said party of the second part, his executors, administrators and assigns, against all and every person and persons whomsoever, lawfully claiming or to claim the same.
IN TESTIMONY WHEREOF, The said party of the first part has hereunto set his
hand and seal this 18th day of January 19 33
Signed, sealed and delivered in presence of   Nick Nummela   [Seal]

JOKIMAKI #6 1909-1929 (NE-NW-14-47-21) County Road 129 in Automba township. (First belonged to District 12 Automba)

The school burned in 1918, was rebuilt in 1919, and consolidated with Kalavala in 1929. The building was used as a granary on the Ray Johnson farm.

Jokimaki School as a granary on the Ray Johnson farm
photo Author's Collection

KONSTI #7 1906-1929 (NW-SW-25-47-20), one mile east of County Road 4.

The school was built in 1906 at a cost of $2,000 and consolidated with Kalevala in 1929. The building was used as a house on the former Otto Eskuri farm. Margaret Cheeseman was the teacher in 1912.

Konsti School, ND,
photo Author's Collection

Pioneer teachers and students of the Kalevala District #16, ND,
1st Row, l to r: Lena Blaha, Millie Novak, Minnie Siemer, Alice Mathison, Mrs. Waino Nummela
2nd Row: Mrs. Axel Aho, Hilda Pietila, Mary Kovanen
3rd Row: Ida Pietila, Ailie Lampel Peura
photo Author's collection

DISTRICT 17 - SELGREN 1895-1910 (SE-NE-24-47-19)
The district was organized January 2, 1895 and consolidated with District #6 August 10, 1910. There was only one school in the district located on Youngren Road.

DISTRICT 18 – SAWYER
Organized on February 11, 1895
Little is known about some of the districts in the county other than their date of organization.

DISTRICT 19 - ATKINSON (Otter Creek) (SE-NW-25-48-18)
UNORGANIZED January 7, 1896
The Otter Creek School was built about 1897 and was the only school in the district. The school was still being used in 1922 and may have been used until the mid 1900s. Carl Anderson was a teacher at the school. It has been used as a church and theatre in recent years.

Atkinson School
CCHS photo

Atkinson students and teachers Miss Hamon and Carl Anderson
photo copy Author's Collection

DISTRICT 20 - SKELTON (NE-NW-35-47-19)

The district was organized January 7, 1896. The district was made up of Skelton (Little), Lind (Hall), and Anderson and was consolidated with Barnum in 1908. Skelton building was there until 1916. After closing it was used for Socialist meetings. John Govan owned the property but not the building, which was moved across road into section 26 on Little Road where the front half became Skelton Town Hall. Winefred McCandless and Lucy Miller were district teachers. Teachers walked the three miles to teach from where they boarded.

Skelton School and students, ND
photo Author's Collection

Skelton School used as the
Skelton Town Hall
photo Author's Collection

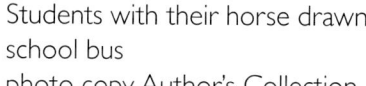

Students with their horse drawn
school bus
photo copy Author's Collection

DISTRICT 21 - EAGLE LAKE #1 1896-1932 (NW-NW-28-48-20)
The district was organized January 13, 1896. The first school was a one room school built in 1896 with additions built in 1906 and 1917.

EAGLE LAKE #2 1932-1964 (NW-NW-33-48-20)
A new school was finished in 1932 one mile south of the first school. The school had four classrooms and a cafeteria with a stage for performances in the basement. Upstairs there was a large teacherage. When attendance was high at the school, four teachers taught eight grades and a semi-graded arrangement of two grades per classroom was used.

PARVIANEN 1919-1932? (SW-SW-36-48-20)
The school was built in 1919, but the date of its closure is unsure. It may have consolidated with Eagle Lake in 1932 when the new school was built. Apparently the Parvianens used the closed school building as a retirement home and it was later moved to Cromwell.

Eagle Lake and Parviainen were the only schools in the district. The district merged with Cromwell-Wright school district, so from 1952-1964 students in grades 1-6 were split between the Wright and Eagle Lake schools until after 1964 when Eagle Lake closed and only the Wright School was used. The second Eagle Lake School is still standing and is currently privately owned.

Source: Ed Manni and Cromwell reunion book

Eagle Lake School photo Author's Collection

Horse drawn Eagle Lake school bus
CCHS photo

68

DISTRICT 22 - MUNSON SCHO0L 1897-1943/4 (NE-SW-14-47-18) later (SE-SW-14-47-18)

The district was organized September 13, 1897. The school was located near Munson Lake.

DISTRICT 23 – HUFFMAN'S CORNERS SCHOOL

The district was organized November 13, 1899 and consolidated with District #8 on June 29, 1911.

DISTRICT 24 - SPENSER SCHOOL 1901-1919 (NE-NE-4-46-19)

The district was organized January 8, 1901 and consolidated with District #6 on April 29, 1919. It was located on Brown Road 1 1/2 to 2 miles west of Barnum.

Spencer School students, early 1900s MLAHS photo

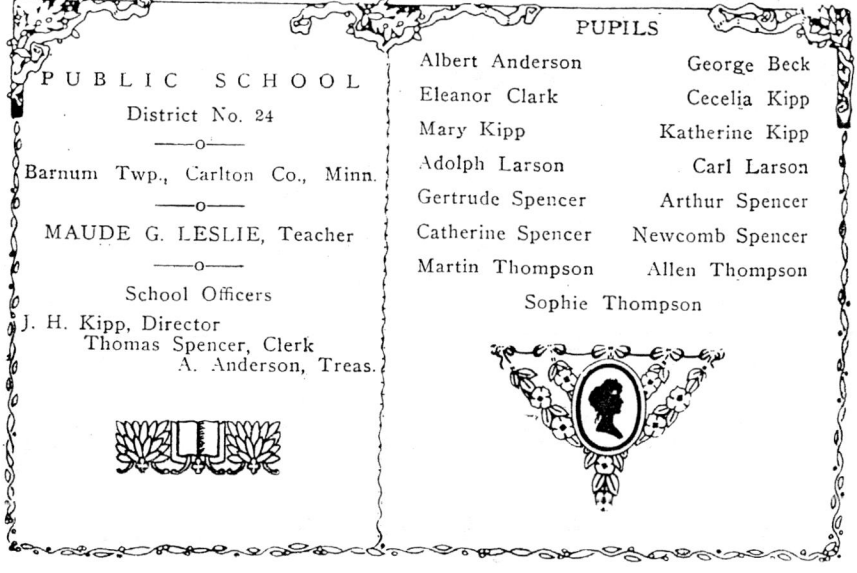

PUBLIC SCHOOL

District No. 24

——o——

Barnum Twp., Carlton Co., Minn.

——o——

MAUDE G. LESLIE, Teacher

——o——

School Officers

J. H. Kipp, Director
Thomas Spencer, Clerk
A. Anderson, Treas.

PUPILS

Albert Anderson	George Beck
Eleanor Clark	Cecelia Kipp
Mary Kipp	Katherine Kipp
Adolph Larson	Carl Larson
Gertrude Spencer	Arthur Spencer
Catherine Spencer	Newcomb Spencer
Martin Thompson	Allen Thompson
Sophie Thompson	

Souvenir Card, Spencer School, ND Author's Collection

DISTRICT 25 - KETTLE RIVER SCHOOL – See Districts 12 and 37
The district was organized June 10, 1901.

McKINLEY (RONKAINEN) 1902-1936 (SE-NW-12-46-20)
February 27, 1902. The school was located on the north side of section 12 near Ronkainen farm on Hwy 12 in Silver Township. Consolidated with Kettle River in 1915, and in 1916 it consolidated with Eckman and Birch Grove to form district 37.

McKinley/Ronkainen School
CCHS photo

McKinley students
Teacher, Linnea Huber
CCHS photo

PAAPANEN SCHOOL (SW-NW-8-46-20) Silver Township, November 18, 1908 Edwin Manni notes that students from Kettle River went to Paapanen as early as 1911, but since there wasn't a bridge crossing the river west of town, students walked across the river on a swinging bridge. Paapanen joined Kettle River in 1915.

MICHAELSON SCHOOL (SE-SE-19-46-20) See District #12
August 14, 1897
The school closed in the mid-1920s and became the Polish National Church. The building is still standing.

ECKMAN SCHOOL (SE-NW-23-46-20) See District #12

After two additions, this was one of the largest schools in the district. The school burned in 1918 and was rebuilt. It was located on Hwy 73 and Carlson Road in the Swedish community there. The community was divided over need for upper grades. Six grades were thought sufficient and 8th grade was barely tolerated, but it became a high school in 1910 and consolidated with Moose Lake in 1936.

BIRCH GROVE (SANDBLOM) (SE-NW-34-46-20) See District #12

October 24, 1908

KETTLE RIVER (SE-NW-9-46-20)

The school was built in 1915 after consolidation with Paapanen and McKinley Schools. It burned in the 1918 fire. School was held in the Marsyla home until the new brick school was built in town by 1920. In 1933 rural students in the district began to be bussed to Moose Lake. In 1948 the 7th and 8th grades were eliminated at Kettle River and students went to Moose Lake. In 1950, Kettle River and Split Rock consolidated with Moose Lake. Elementary school continued in Kettle River into the 1970s, but eventually students in all grades began attending Moose Lake. Nemadji Pottery was using the abandoned school building as a warehouse when it burned down in 1991.

Kettle River school, ca. 1918
photo Author's Collection

K. R. School before the fire

A Student Remembers...

"Walked to the bus 1/2 mile, rode about 15 miles— no heater. We stopped at the Kettle River store—the side that faced the stove warmed up, but quickly we were cold again."

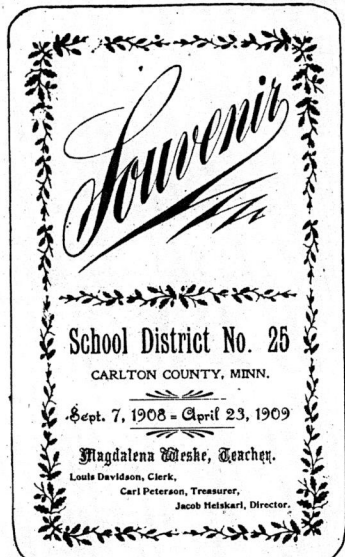

District #25 Souvenir card, 1909
Author's Collection

Kettle River School
photo copy Author's
Collection

Kettle River School
Grades 1 and 2, 1937
Teacher, Miss Budd
MLAHS photo

DISTRICT 26 - NILSEN/CENTER SCHOOL
The district was organized June 9, 1902.

BESEMAN TOWNSHIP

CENTER SCHOOL (NE-NE 21-49-21)
The school was located four miles north of Wright from 1927-1945. Students went to Wright after closing.

NORTON SCHOOL (SW-SW-7-49-21?) Exact location uncertain.
Norton was one room school in District 26. In the early days children who lived more than a mile away were transported by horse drawn rigs and later by automobiles.

NILSEN SCHOOL (BRENNICK) (NE-NE2-48-21)
It was built before 1912 on one acre of donated land and was also called Brennick. It was located on Old Hwy 2 about two miles east of Wright. It closed in 1939 and students were bussed to either Cromwell or Wright. In 1946 the building was sold and torn down to reuse the lumber. The last three teachers were Margaret Johnson, Anne Madsen, and Ruth Calhoun.

LAKEVIEW TOWNSHIP

LAKESIDE SCHOOL (SW-NE-19-48-21 on 1927 map)
(NW-NE-19-48-21 on 1935 map)
Starting in 1906 school was held in the Isaac Walli home. Lakeside School was built about 1908 and was located 2 1/2 miles east of Wright. A second room was added to the school in 1928. At one point 90 students attended the two-room school. It closed in 1940 when students were bussed to Wright. In 1948 the school district gave the school to the Lakeside Community Club.

LINCOLN SCHOOL
A school appears on the 1914 map at NW-SE-22-48-21. Could this be Lincoln School?

RIVERSIDE (SOUTH) (WALIMAA) (SW-SE-29-48-21)
The school was built in 1923 to accommodate the large enrollment at the Lakeside School.

DISTRICT 27 - SCANLON SCHOOL (SW-SW-19-49-16)

The district was organized July 14, 1902. The first school was a six-room frame school built in 1902 on top of the hill that leads down to the west bank of the St. Louis River. It burned in 1904 and a new identical school was built on present day Washington Avenue near the intersection with Hwy 45. This school lasted until 1952 when a new brick school was built. The old building was torn down and the site sold to the Bethel Lutheran Church. The brick school on Dewey Avenue is now used as a city hall and community center and Scanlon children attend Cloquet schools.

Scanlon school, students, and teachers, 1905, CCHS photo

The second Scanlon School
CCHS photo

Scanlon students, 1940
CCHS photo by Olaf Olson

DISTRICT 28 – CORONA (SE-SW-7-48-19?)

The district was organized on August 10, 1903. Little information is available about this school and the location is debatable. One report says there were a foundation and steps of the school in section 7 at the Strandberg and Corona Roads.

DISTRICT 29 - BEEHIVE SCHOOL 1903-1938 (NW-NW-3-47-19, 2nd School)

The district was organized September 14, 1903. There were actually two Beehive School buildings that operated side-by-side with their dates of operation overlapping. At least for a period, the older 4 grades were taught at the old school and the younger 4 grades at the new school. It was named because the teacher said children sounded like a hive of bees. The first building burned and the second remains as a community center west of Mahtowa.

The "new" Beehive School, built 1915, photo Author's Collection

Students at Beehive School, ca. 1926-27, photo Author's Collection

DISTRICT 30 – BENNY PETERSON 1903-1912 (Section 1 or 2-46-18)

The district was organized November 9, 1903 and consolidated with District #8 in 1912. See District #8.

Benny Peterson School building in February, 2002. It was moved from its original site on one side of Deer Park Road to the other and used as a private residence.
photo Author's Collection

DISTRICT 31 – CLEAR CREEK SCHOOL (PIONEER SCHOOL, later JONES) in CLEAR CREEK TOWNSHIP (SW-SW-11-46-17)

The district was organized November 14, 1904 and a school was built around 1915. Clear Creek was also called Pioneer or Jones School. It burned in 1920 and was rebuilt as Jones slightly to the east nearer to Silver Brook. Fire was the fate of many schools. It closed in 1935. Graduations were held in Barnum. The building was moved to Holyoke and used as a garage and town hall. The first teacher was Leona Lull. She had twelve students. Inez Anderson taught there also.

Clear Creek School, ca. 1930-31, "The Little Yellow Schoolhouse"
CCHS photo

DISTRICT 32 – HOLYOKE

The district was organized January 3, 1905.

HOLYOKE TOWN SCHOOL (SW-NE–17- 46-16)

The school was built in 1905 when the town was organized. It was just west of Park. It was open 1905-1954 for grades 1-8. There was a 9th grade class one year. Some students went to upper grades in Carlton and others went to stay in Duluth to finish high school at Denfeld.

HOLYOKE SOUTHSIDE (NW-SW-28-46-16)

The land for the South School was purchased in 1920 from Nick Johnson and construction of the school began. Previously students in the south area had been bussed to the Holyoke town school. Gertrude Flavelle was the first teacher at South School. She taught there for four years and lived at the home of Herman Zinter. Parents of the students of South School were reimbursed for providing transportation for their children. Bussing was in operation in 1936. Older children were bussed to Carlton. The school closed in 1948 or 49. The students were again transported to the town school of Holyoke. The South School building continued to be used for social get-togethers.

Hogan's Mirror
Nov. 15, 1926

HOLYOKE

The following pupils at the South school had perfect attendance for the month of October.

Ambrose Culliton.
Rose Fabrello.
Elizabeth Renz.
Gerda Semerau.
Margaret Semerau.
Darl Switzer.

Hogan's Mirror
December 15, 1926

SOUTH SCHOOL, HOLYOKE

The following had perfect attendance for the month of November:

Earl Ball.
Irvin Ball.
Margaret Ball.
Ambrose Culliton.
Rose Fabrello.
Agnes Menne.
Bernard Menne.
Milton Persons.
Gerda Semerau.
Margaret Semerau.
Darl Switzer.

A student remembers...

"The school nurse checked teeth, head, throat, etc. Sometimes she even removed a tooth.
I was always scared to death of her."

DISTRICT 33 – CLEAR CREEK

The district was organized July 12, 1909. It consolidated with District # 13.

DISTRICT 34 - SPLIT ROCK TOWNSHIP

The district was organized October 3, 1910.

SOBELESKI/LINCOLN (March 22, 1915) (NE-NW-9-46-21)

The school burned in the 1918 fire and was rebuilt and renamed Lincoln. It closed in 1948 and was consolidated with Moose Lake.

SHUSTA/WILSON SCHOOL (July 26, 1915) SE-SE-19-46-21)

The land was purchased from Lyman Brandt for $35. A list of teachers includes Madius Anderson (1920-21), Alice Cronstrom Haverson (1926-30), and Bernice Gresczyk (1947-48). The school closed and was consolidated with Moose Lake in 1950.

JOHNSON SCHOOL (December 30, 1915) (SE-SE-11-46-21)

Alfred and Jensina Johnson gave land for the school in December of 1915. The school burned in the 1918 fire and was rebuilt in 1922. It closed in 1945 when it was consolidated with Kettle River and later Moose Lake.

WASHINGTON (June 21, 1926) (SW-SW-23-46-21) (Across from St. Joseph's Church)

The land was obtained from William Suchoski. In 1948, the 7th and 8th grades were in Moose Lake. Grades 1 – 6 were at Washington until 1950 when there was a consolidation with Moose Lake and then the school was used for grades 1 – 3 until the school closed in 1958. The building became the Split Rock Town Hall until it burned in November of 1985. Some teachers were Walma Waisanen, Bernice ?, and Mary Suchoski (1948-1949). Serving on the school board in the 1930s were John Maniak, John Butkiewicz, and William Suchoski.

Washington School, which became Split Rock Town Hall, ND photo copy Author's Collection

KACHINSKI 1896-1916 (SE- SE-21-46-21)

The school was built on a tract of land given to the district by the St. Paul-Duluth Railroad in October, 1896. The school burned in 1916 and school was then held in a log Catholic Church for the remainder of the academic year. The school was apparently not rebuilt. Martha Larson was a teacher.

Kachinski students and teacher Margaret Spencer Peters, 1906 photo Author's Collection

DISTRICT 35 – LONE PINE, HANSON (SW-SE-26-48-17)

The district was organized November 6, 1911. Dissolved into District #3, Carlton. See District #3.

DISTRICT 36 – BLACKHOOF VALLEY SCHOOL (NE-NW-7-47-17)

The district was organized July 14, 1913. The school was constructed in 1916 to accommodate an influx of students that made the Pleasant View School too small. The school was built on land sold to the district by Hjalmer and Kathryn Flodin and was a two-room school with indoor plumbing and a furnace. In March of 1929, the school burned in a fire ignited by sparks from the furnace landing on the roof. Area residents managed to save all of the school's furnishings. The school term was finished out in the Flodin home. A new school was built and operated until 1961 using the furniture salvaged from the old school. The building still stands on County Road 5 and is used as a community center.

The first Blackhoof Valley School, built in 1916 and burned in 1929. photo copy Author's Collection

DISTRICT 37 – BIRCH GROVE/SANDBLOM

See District #25 and District #12.
The district was organized August 1, 1916 and consolidated with District #3 October 27, 1936.

DISTRICT 38 – BLACKHOOF, RIVERSIDE (NE-SE-15-47-17)

The district was organized August 7, 1917 and the school built in October of 1917. Located across from the Matten residence on County Road 103. Documented by Florence Carlson.

Riverside School, ND
photo Author's Collection

DISTRICT 39 – LAKESIDE (SW-NE-19-48-21)

The district was organized February 4, 1919. Students originally walked to Wright until 1906 when a teacher taught in the home of Isaac Walli. A school was built in 1908 and an addition was made to the school in 1928. It closed in 1938 or 39 and in the fall of 1940 the children went to Lincoln Elementary in Wright. In 1948 the school district gave the school building to the Lakeside Community Club.

Teachers: Carl Johnson, Joyce Groth, Wayne Bradford, Shirley Walli, Charles Kisler, Orson Illstrup, Donald Bushey, Jean Peterson, Helen Wanous, Jimmy Cornforth

Lakeside School as a Community Club
photo Author's Collection

Lakeside students and teacher,
1920, photo Author's Collection

RIVERSIDE SOUTH/WALIMAA, (SW-SE-29-48-21)

The school was built ca. 1923 to accommodate increasing numbers of students at the Lakeside School. It was merged with Cromwell in 1965.
Teachers: Addia Ranta, Lillian Mannelin, George Matkala, Shirley Walli.

DISTRICT 40 – BARKER

The district was organized November 4, 1919 and was dissolved and annexed to District 15. See District #15.

DISTRICT 41 – HOLYOKE SOUTHSIDE

The district was organized November 4, 1919. See District #32.

Holyoke School, ND, CCHS photo

DISTRICT 42 – WATSON (SE-SW-13-48-19)

The district was organized December 7, 1920. This small school was located in Corona Township and probably closed around 1937.

Watson School and students
photo Author's Collection

DISTRICT 43 – PARK LAKE

The district was organized October 7, 1921. See District #14.

DISTRICT 44 – CLEAR CREEK/JONES (SW-SW-11-46-17)

The district was organized February 7, 1922 and dissolved October 5, 1935. The Clear Creek school evidently was built ca. 1915 and burned in 1920 and was rebuilt slightly to the east nearer to Silver Brook. (SW-SE-11-46-17).

RAYMOND, SOPER (NE-SE-28-46-17)

The Holyoke 4-H project says that the Soper School was located 1 1/2 miles south of Karl VanGuilder's home. Its dates of operation are uncertain.

DISTRICT 45 – HOLYOKE EAST/PUGSLEY, FOXBORO
(SW-SW-1-46-16) perhaps school moved to (SW-SE-1-46-16)

The district was organized March 6, 1923. In 1908 the first teacher was Lydia Carlson. Before and after Pugsley School, children went to Foxboro, Wisconsin. When Foxboro began charging out of state tuition, students were bussed into Holyoke to the town school. The school closed in 1938.

DISTRICT 46 – PERCH LAKE, BERGMAN 1912-1936?
(SE-NE-11-49-18)

The district was organized July 9, 1923. A small log school house must have been replaced by a second Bergman School probably about 1915.

First Bergman School
CCHS photo

Bergman School students
CCHS photo

Second Bergman School, ca. 1915
CCHS photo

DISTRICT 47 – BLACKHOOF (NW-NW-34-47-17)

The district was organized September 4, 1923. The school was built around 1914-15 and closed about 1939. Students then went to Barnum.

Blackhoof School, ca. 1931-32
photo Author's Collectiion

DISTRICT 48 – UNORGANIZED FOND DU LAC RESERVATION
BIG LAKE 1925/26-mid 1930s (SW-NW-22-49-18)

Parents petitioned to have a school built for their children. Most of the students were children of white settlers of various nationalities and one Indian family.

KATTMAN (NE-SE-26-49-18)

It is documented that the Kattman School was first located in an old abandoned sawmill which was used until the Bergman School opened in 1912. Martin Kotiranta had blueprints for the Kattman School and built a model of it for the Carlton County Historical Society. Its history and exact location through the years remains unknown.

Kattman School, 1927
CCHS photo

DITCHBANK SCHOOL (SE-SE-17-49-18)

Little information is known of this school. According to Kay Monson, a school existed on Ditchbank Road.

RESERVATION SCHOOLS

Two "day" schools existed on the Fond du Lac Reservation in the later 1800s and early 1900s. These schools were overseen by a federal Indian Agent and not the county superintendent. Reports submitted to the Indian Agents outline problems with inadequate buildings, equipment, and supplies. Malnutrition, poverty, and poor attendance made schooling difficult for the students.

FOND-DU-LAC DAY SCHOOL
Old School: Built 1883, (NW-NE-SW-10-49-17)—New School: Built 1896, (SW-SW-NW-10-49-17)

The Reservation day school was located at the old Fond du Lac village site on the bluff of the St. Louis River between Holy Family Church and Jarvi Road. The school was only 1/2 mile from the old church. The school closed early in 1919. The use of the word "Day" school was probably a reflection of the Indian boarding school days. Since this was a reservation school, it was not overseen by the county superintendent, but by Indian Agents employed by the federal government. It was fraught with problems, such as poor attendance, poor water, lack of rudimentary equipment such as desks and books, poverty, malnutrition, and diseases. Attendance was impacted by the cycle of traditional life such as harvesting maple sugar and wild rice. There was an emphasis was on "industrial training." This school probably burned in the 1918 fire, since most buildings burned in the Fond du Lac village.

NORMANTOWN DAY SCHOOL **Between 1889 and 1893 – between 1918 and 1922 (NW-SW-33-49-18)**

A narrative in the CCHS files states that "a one-room school known as the Normantown Day School was located at Sawyer near Big Lake from the early 1890s until 1919." There may have been a temporary shut-down of the school around 1912 (perhaps because of a lack of students?). By 1922 students in the area could attend the Sawyer school, which opened in 1922 and served both Indian and non-Indian children.

FOND DU LAC OJIBWE SCHOOL, **49 University Road, Cloquet**

The Fond du Lac Ojibwe School opened in 1980 for grades 7-12 with an enrollment of 20. Grades K-6 were added in 1988. New school buildings have been built for both the Ojibwe School and Head Start programs. Along with the required curriculum as in public schools, the Fond du Lac Ojibwe School offers Ojibwe language and cultural curriculum in all subject areas.

Sources: Dan Anderson, Fond du Lac Education, and Carlton County Historical Society files

Fond du Lac Day School
students and teacher
CCHS photo from St. John's
Abbey Archives

Diagram of the
Normantown
School area, 1895,
CCHS files

FOND-DU-LAC RESERVATION,

Cloquet, Minn. Nov. 8 th, 1895.

Lieut.W.A.Mercer,U.S.Ind.,

Ashland, Wis.

Sir:--

In compliance with your requwst, I have made Digram, showing
the NORMAN TOWN SCHOOL PROPERTY, on the Fond-du-Lac Reservation, as
described below.

Section-32, Town-49, Range-18.   Section-33, Town-49, Range-18.

Big Lake

32

7

21.50

6

33

20.00 a.
Lot 1.

37.80 a.
2

23.75
3

41.60

30.80
5.

4.

--School Building- 24 X 30,

--Dwelling House for Teacher- 16 X 24, addition- 12 X 16.

--Wood-shed- 16 X 24,

--Well,

--Out-houses. 4 X 6,

Additional Farmer.

86

PINE COUNTY SCHOOLS

DISTRICT 11 WINDEMERE TOWNSHIP SCHOOLS

School district 11 was organized in 1889. It had four rural schools called A, B, C, and D. In 1885 the A school was built on the west end of Island Lake. The B school was on the southeast shore of Sturgeon Lake. The C school was also called 11. It burned and was rebuilt. D school was also called the Sands. Myrtle Nystrom was the last teacher in C school from 1968-1970. The building was sold to Windemere Township for a town hall.

Windemere School C
MLAHS photo

DISTRICT 19 BIRCH CREEK TOWNSHIP

Birch Creek School #19 was a log building. Many students lived up to eight miles from school, which was located in the SW corner of section 24. The second school was organized in 1897 and was called the Ten Post School. Another school was built in section 19. It was known as the West School and was in section 33. It was two stories and used for many community activities. It was later torn down. In 1906 district 27 was divided and Ten Post moved one mile east. The resulting divisions eventually put children no more than two miles from school. District 107 was the Birch Creek School. The Sunny Beach School was located in District 83 in 1909.

DISTRICT 107 DENHAM SCHOOL

School began in 1915 and the building burned in the 1918 fires. A reunion was held in 1997.

Denham School and students, 1917
photo Author's Collection

DISTRICT 19 STURGEON LAKE

District 84 section 7 was organized in 1909 called 84.
It was originally on section 8.
District 96 section # 28 Cherry Grove.
Lincoln School section 10
Unidentified school 9
Nickerson #86 was built in 1909.

DISTRICT 18 KERRICK SCHOOL

Kerrick School 1916
Duquette School #18, Section 24, organized in 1889, burned in 1921.
Oak Lake #95 1916, consolidated in 1970 with Askov.
Kerrick IDS 566
Sunny Hill School #9
Oak Grove School #88
Beaver #1565 up to 1970

AITKIN COUNTY SCHOOLS

Larson School, burned 1918
Wilson 2 1/2 miles from Denham
Riverside
Green Valley
Rice River District 18
Sunnyside District 18
Ronald

1929

The Graduating Class

cordially invites you and your
friends to attend the

Eleventh Annual
Commencement

of the ungraded schools of Carlton County

to be held at the High School

Barnum, Minnesota, on

Friday, July 12, at 2:00 o'clock P. M.

PROGRAM

Forenoon, Begins at 10 O'clock

Commencement

Afternoon Program Begins at 2:00 O'clock

Entrance March_____Nora Grindy
Invocation_____Rev. E. A. Cooke
Carlton County Creed_____Graduates
Song_____Scanlon Graduates
Reading_____Alice Mathison, Mahtowa
Reading—"An Aspiring Dishwasher"_____
_____Jenny Wesa, Wright, Dist. 39
Song_____Mahtowa Graduates
Reading—"Nice Da-da"_____Viola Sarvela, Kettle River
Reading—"Jimmy Studies Geography"___Lauri Hill, Sawyer
Reading—"God Remembers"_____Vivian Clark, Holyoke
Duet—"Remember Now Thy Creator", Alice and Mary Olgren
Address_____
Supt. A. L. Winterquist, Town of Thomson Schools, Cloquet
Song_____Mahtowa Graduates
Introduction of winners of Declamatory and Spelling Contests and awarding of diplomas_____
_____Nora A. Nilsen, County Superintendent
Duet_____Alice and Mary Olgren

The readings above are given by those who won out in the sectional declamatory contests. Judges will select one to represent this county at the state contest. Two spellers will compete for honors at the state spelling contest.

CLASS ROLL

DIST.	TEACHER	GRADUATES
2	May Beattie	Ruby Swenson Carlton
4	Edythe Putzke	Juanita Rogers Sandy Lake
		Robert Haglund
		Kenneth Nelson
		Marjorie Spangle
5	Freda Mathison	Elsie Chell Mahtowa
		Melvin Johnson
		Grace Osborne
		Rudolph Peterson
		Evelyn Runnberg
		Eleanor Peterson
		Esther Nordin
		Pearl Nelson
		Florence Munter
		Alice Mathison
		Beatrice Brindos
		Earl Carlson
		Clifford Thompson
9	Adah Carlson	Arnold Johnson Praefke
11	R. Leroy Ewoldsen	Doris Guitare Wrenshall wright
		Carl Vernon Stenson
		Margaret Johnson
		John Dearborn
		Marvin Bern
		Hilary Zoerb
		Carl Lundquist
		Henry Hjulstad

CLASS ROLL

DIST.	TEACHER	GRADUATES
14	Rose Zacher	Senia Mannila
		Eino Kamunen
		Elma Salmi
		George Niemi
		Willie Jaskari
		Olive Wheatley
		Helen Zacher
		Rachel Hill
		Edward Hill
		Esther DuFault
		Viola Sandgren
16	Ethel Emilson	Viena Peterson Kalevala
	Helen Harmala	Walter Isaacson
		Mayme Isaacson
		Heimo Holm
	Percy Pringle	Tauno Pietila
		Hugo Metso
		Harry Metso
		Albert Ketola

1929 Commencement Program for Carlton County ungraded schools

Bibliography & Recommended Reading

The files of the Carlton County Historical Society and the Moose Lake Area Historical Society contain much information about the schools of Carlton County. Their libraries also house copies of local history books that have been used to compile this history and might not otherwise be readily available.

Almquist, Patty. *Denham.* self-published, 2009

Anderson, David E. *Moose Lake Area History.* Moose Lake, 1965.

Beck, Bennett A. *Brief History of the Pioneers of the Cromwell Minnesota Area.* 2nd ed. Carlton County Historical Society, Cloquet, 2001.

Benson, Helen. *Have No Fear, Wright is Still Here!!!!!!: Memories Compiled by Helen Benson.* 2000.

Book of Mahtowa: Before and After the Turn of the Century: Willie Newmans Historical Old Time Engravings. ND

Carlson, Florence. Interview with Joseph Malkovich. July 13, 2001. Carlton County Historical Society.

Carlton County Centennial: 1857 – 1957, Official Souvenir Program. 1957.

Carlton County Historical Society Rural Education Project Questionnaires. 2001. (On file at Carlton County Historical Society.)

Carroll, Francis M. *Crossroads in Time: A History of Carlton County Minnesota.* Carlton County Historical Society, Cloquet, MN, 1987.

Carroll, Francis M. and Marlene Wisuri and the Carlton History Committee. *Carlton Chronicles.* Carlton County Historical Society, Cloquet, 2006.

Carroll, Francis M. and Marlene Wisuri. *Reflections of Our Past: A Pictorial History of Carlton County, Minnesota.* Donning Company, Virginia Beach, VA, 1997.

Cromwell All School Reunion: 100 Years, 1891 – 1991. July 1991.

Eller, Dawn-Marie. *Always Onward: Barnum, The First 100 Years.* Star Gazette, Moose Lake, MN, 1989.

Froberg, Mary. Interview with Joseph Malkovich. July 16, 2001. Carlton County Historical Society.

Hanson, Nancy. *Fire Beast.* Moose Lake Area Historical Society, Moose Lake, 1994.

Johnson, Lois. *Sturgeon Lake 1901-2001*. Centennial Committee of Sturgeon Lake, 2001.

Kalevala School Reunion Pamphlet. August 1, 1981.

Lehet, Betty Lampell. *Kalevala Schools 1894-2008*. self-published, 2008.

Lehet, Betty Lampell. *Kettle River: A Look at the Past 100 Years*. self-published, 2009.

Lehet, Betty Lampell and Nancy Hanson, *1918 Fire Stories*. Moose Lake Area Historical Society, Moose Lake, 2003.

Luukkonen, Larry and Marlene Wisuri. *A Hometown Album: Cloquet's Centennial Story*. Carlton County Historical Society, Cloquet, 2004.

Mahlberg, Roy W. *The Wright Place: A Brief History of Its Settlers*. Savage Press, Superior, WI, 1997.

Manni, Edwin E. *Kettle River, Automba, Kalevala, and Surrounding Area: History*. 1978.

Mattinen, John A. *History of the Thomson Farming Area*. Trans. Richard Impola. Northwestern Publishing Co. New York Mills, MN, 1935, trans., Carlton County Historical Society, Cloquet, 2000.

Mattinen, Ray. Interview with Ed Sunnarborg and Charlie Johnson. Date unknown. Carlton County Historical Society. Original tape at Esko Historical Society.

Moose Lake Area History: Volume II, 1918 to the Present. 1989.

Naslund, Alan. Interview with Joseph Malkovich. July 9, 2001. Carlton County Historical Society.

Niemi, Ruby. Interview with Joseph Malkovich. July 17, 2001. Carlton County Historical Society.

Overlie, Ladean. Interview with Joseph Malkovich. July 18, 2001. Carlton County Historical Society.

Piipo-Lambert, Carol Illikainen. *Firebeast: The Fires of 1918*. Moose Lake Area Historical Society, Moose Lake, 1994.

Reed, Daniel. *Automba: A Study of a Finnish Timber Boomtown*. Automba Publishing, Automba, 1990.

Sheetz, Don and Doris. Interview with Joseph Malkovich. June 30, 2001. Carlton County Historical Society.

Swanson, Esther. Interview with Joseph Malkovich. July 12, 2001. Carlton County Historical Society.

Swanson, S. Hjalmar. *A History of Mahtowa: with Additional Material by Willie Newman.* Carlton County Historical Society, Cloquet, 2005.

Waseen, Russell. *The Big Lake Community: The Way It Was.* 1992.

Waseen, Russell. *History of Waseen's Green Acres.* 1984.

Watters, Ira. Interview with Joseph Malkovich. July 3, 2001. Carlton County Historical Society.

Wold, Don. *The Other West Side Story.* 1989.

Maps

1914 County Commissioners Map, found at Carlton County Land Office, Carlton.

1927 Carlton County Plat Book, photocopies on file at the Carlton County Historical Society.

1935 "Handschu" Map, found at Carlton County Land Office, Carlton.

1994 Carlton County Plat Book.

"Carlton County, Minnesota: Schools Then and Now" Made by Nancy Hanson for the Carlton County Fair, as of August 2001 at the Carlton County Historical Society, Cloquet.

"Rural Schools of Carlton County's Past" Made by Joe Malkovich, August 2001. At the Carlton County Historical Society, Cloquet.

THE MINNESOTA
STATE HIGH SCHOOL BOARD

1914

This Certifies, That Emil O. Peterson

has passed an examination in Eighth Grade Comp. having

written the same in the Public Schools of Carlton County

and attained a standing of Passed.

Superintendent of Public Instruction
EXAMINER

INDEX

Lull, Mrs. Clem 21
Lundberg, Al 59

Madsen, Anne 73
Mahtowa 10, 20, 35, 36, 75
Maijala, Jenny 53
Majewski, Stephanie 21
Maki, Martha 20
Maki, Mrs. 34
Maniak, John 78
Mankato 7
Mannelin, Lillian 81
Manni, Edwin 70
Mansikka 11, 61, 62, 63
Mansikka, Joe 63
Martin, Aune 62
Mathiason 63
Mathison, Alice 65
Mathison, Freda 21
Matkala, George 81
Mattson, Alex 63
Mattson, Arvi 53
Mattson, Arvo 53
Mattson, Charlie 53
Mattson, Waino 53
Maunu 10, 25
Maygren, Eddy 49
McCandless, Winefred 67
McIntyre, Mrs. 61
McKinley 11, 12, 21, 48, 60, 70, 71
Michaelson 11, 12, 52, 70
Michaelson, John 52
Mietinen, Dagmar 20, 61
Miller, Etta 53
Miller, Lucy 67
Monson, Kay 84
Moorhead 7
Moose Lake 10, 14, 15, 31-34, 49, 54, 61, 71, 78
Moose Lake Implement 49
Moser, Chris 49
Mossberg, Robert 32
Mud Creek 11, 20, 49, 50
Munson 12, 20, 69

Nasi 11, 63, 64
Naslund, Al 35
Neimela, Mike 63

Nels Johnson 10, 25
Nelson, Ernest 35
Nelson, Helen 21
Nemadji 10, 46, 47
Nemadji Pottery 71
Newman, Willie 35, 37
Newton, Erwin 55
Nickerson #86 88
Niemi, Ruby 30
Nilsen 12, 20, 51, 73
Nilsen, Nora 9
Nilsen, Rev. Nils 9, 31
Nordberg 11, 64
Normal school 7, 15
Normantown Day 14, 85, 86
Norton 12, 51, 73
Nothern Pacific Junction 28
Novak, Millie 65
Nummela, Mrs. Waino 65
Nummela, Nick 64
Nynas, Wendla 53
Nystrom, Myrtle 87

Oak Grove #88 88
Oak Lake #95 88
Olesen, Peter 42
Olson, Elaine 57
Olson, Gust 53
Olson, Hilda 20
Olson, Ludwig 53, 63
Olson, Nora 20
Otilla 10, 25
Otter Creek 12, 66
Otteson, Helen 20
Owen, Ella 24

Paapanen 12, 70, 71
Paine, Daisy 55
Paine, Lydia 55
Pantsar 10, 25
Park Lake 11, 13, 21, 36, 57, 58, 82
Parvianen 68
Paulson, Ted 46
Perch Lake 14, 16, 82
Peters, Florence 20, 59
Peters, Margaret Spencer 79
Peterson, Eddie 53
Peterson, Esther 53
Peterson, Jean 80

Peterson, Mr. 54
Peura, Ailie Lampel 65
Philips, Miss 40
Pickerel Lake 11, 50
Pietala, Hilda 65
Pietala, Ida 65
Pietila, Axel 59
Pine County 87
Pioneer 30, 35, 76
Pleasant Valley 10, 11, 48
Pleasant View 10, 30, 35, 59, 60
Polish National Church 70
Praefke 11, 20, 59, 60
Progress 16
Putzke, Grace 21

Ranta, Addia 81
Ranua 11, 63
Rautio, Lempi 62
Raymond 13, 21, 82
Red Clover Twnsp 11, 16, 56
Reed, Matt 52, 59
Rice River 88
Riverside (South) 12, 73, 81
Riverside 88
Rogers, Ella 63
Rohlf, Ernst 49
Ronald 88
Ronkainen 6, 12, 70
Ronkainen, Thomas 52
Rudabeck, John 64

Sacred Heart Church 52
Salem Lutheran Church 35, 57
Salo 11, 61, 63
Sandblom 11, 12, 13, 54, 71, 80
Sands 87
Sandstrom, Ella 63
Sandy Lake 10, 20, 35
Sawyer 11, 12, 16, 21, 28, 57, 66
Scanlon 12, 20, 74
Schauland, Katherine 21
Scott, Dorothy 59
Selgren 12, 66
Shaw, William 24
Shusta 13, 78
Siemer, Minnic 10, 49, 65
Siltanen, Aili 20
Silver 13, 16

ABOUT THE AUTHOR...

Nancy Hanson was raised in Minneapolis, Minnesota. She graduated in education from the University of Minnesota and taught in Minnesota and California schools. She has written six books on genealogy and local history.

Nancy lives with her husband Robert in Barnum, Minnesota, where she continues to do research for individuals and organizations.